Luxury for him

Lujo para él

Luxe pour lui

Editorial coordination:
Simone Schleifer

Editor:
Cristina Paredes, Montse Borràs

Texts:
Cristina Paredes, Montse Borràs, Julio Fajardo

Editorial assistant:
Esther Moreno, Paz Diman

English translation:
Rachel Chaundler/Cillero&deMotta

French translation:
Claire Pierry/Cillero&deMotta

English proofreading:
Elizabeth Jackson/Cillero&deMotta

French proofreading:
Alban Gourmelen/Cillero&deMotta

Art director:
Mireia Casanovas Soley

Design and layout:
Laura Millán, Claudia Martínez Alonso

Editorial proyect:
2008 © LOFT Publications
Via Laietana 32, 4º Of. 92
08003 Barcelona, España
Tel.: +34 932 688 088
Fax: +34 932 687 073
loft@loftpublications.com
www.loftpublications.com

ISBN: 978-84-96936-28-7

Printed in China

Luxury for him

Lujo para él

Luxe pour lui

LOFT

CONTENTS ÍNDICE SOMMAIRE

INTRODUCTION

What is luxury? What objects, places, goods are considered luxurious? Luxury tends to be associated with excess, with unnecessary belongings. However, luxurious objects are also unique and special with a value beyond numbers. Although luxurious items are magnificent, rich, or even excessive, they always have a demonstrable value. Luxury can manifest itself in different ways and objects of desire differ from person to person. Although the parameters of what is considered to be luxurious vary greatly, luxurious items always have excellent quality, are exclusive limited editions which tend to be the most technologically advanced within their category. Elegance and distinction have various interpretations, but in all cases, the degree of excellence and quality in the materials and objects is what distinguishes genuine luxury from opulence that is lacking in content.

In a consumer society such as the West, where basic necessities are covered for the majority of the population, people strive to rise above others and somehow be special. Individuality, difference and exclusivity are sought after. Any object, if it is different and possesses a high quality and excellence may be an object of luxury. Yachts and sailboats, private jets and latest generation electronic equipment are all sought after in order to mark differences. Not only physical objects are luxurious; every day more experiences can be catalogued as luxurious.

For executives with an intensive work load, luxury consists of enjoying free time with family or friends. For those who are lovers of driving, an object of luxury could be a fast and powerful sports car. For those in search for emotions, an impressive sailboat can push them to sail the seas in search of adventure.

In this book an attempt has been made to compile luxury objects from different fields. It exhibits classical sports cars, motorcycles, yachts and private jets on its pages. Faraway destinations and small and exclusive objects, almost of cult status, can also be enjoyed. All to satisfy the desires of lovers of luxury.

Introducción

¿Qué es el lujo? ¿Qué objetos, lugares y bienes se consideran lujosos? Normalmente, el lujo se asocia con lo superfluo, con todo aquello que no es necesario para vivir. También es cierto que los objetos lujosos son únicos, especiales y con un valor que va más allá de lo puramente económico. Lujoso es todo aquello que se define como magnífico, rico, incluso excesivo, y de una valía demostrada. El lujo puede manifestarse de distintas formas, y cada persona tiene por objeto de deseo algo diferente. Los parámetros de lo que se considera lujoso difieren según la personalidad de cada uno. Habitualmente, se estiman lujosos aquellos objetos que tienen una calidad excelente, que son exclusivos, de edición limitada, y que suelen ser los más avanzados tecnológicamente dentro de su categoría. La elegancia y la distinción tienen varias lecturas, pero, en cualquier caso, un cierto grado de excelencia y calidad en los materiales y los objetos es lo que separa el auténtico lujo de una opulencia vacía en contenido.

En una sociedad de consumo como la occidental, en la cual las necesidades básicas están cubiertas para la mayoría de la población, se busca distinguirse de los demás y ser especial. Se busca la particularidad, la diferencia, la exclusividad. Cualquier elemento, si es distinto y posee gran calidad y excelencia, puede ser un artículo de lujo. Desde los yates y los veleros hasta los aviones privados o los aparatos electrónicos de última generación, todos ellos son deseados por la distinción que implican. Pero el lujo no sólo atañe a los objetos concretos; cada vez son más las experiencias que pueden definirse como lujosas.

Para los ejecutivos con un fuerte ritmo de trabajo, el lujo consistiría en disfrutar del tiempo libre con la familia o con amigos. Para aquellos que son amantes de la conducción, un objeto de lujo sería un veloz y potente coche deportivo. Para quienes buscan emociones, un velero impresionante puede empujarlos a surcar los mares en busca de aventuras.

En este libro se ha intentado reunir objetos de lujo de diferentes ámbitos. Aquí se muestran desde clásicos coches deportivos hasta motocicletas, yates y aviones privados. También se puede disfrutar de destinos lejanos, así como de pequeños y exclusivos objetos, casi de culto. Todo para satisfacer los deseos de los amantes del lujo.

Introduction

Qu'est-ce que le luxe ? Quels sont les objets, les destinations ou les biens qui peuvent être considérés comme luxueux ? Habituellement, le luxe est associé au superflu et à tout ce qui n'est pas essentiel pour vivre. Mais les objets de luxe sont aussi uniques, singuliers et dotés d'une valeur qui va au-delà de ce qui est purement économique. Le luxe est synonyme de magnificence, de richesse, d'exclusivité et possède une valeur reconnue et indiscutable. Il peut se manifester sous diverses formes et les objets de désir sont propres à chaque individu. Ainsi, les paramètres qui définissent ce qu'est le luxe sont à chaque fois différents. Mais habituellement ces objets répondent à des critères de perfection, d'exclusivité, d'édition limitée et ce sont généralement des objets dotés des toutes dernières technologies. Le degré d'élégance et de distinction n'est pas toujours équivalent, cependant, tous les matériaux utilisés possèdent un certain niveau d'excellence et de qualité : ces objets permettent de faire la différence entre ce qu'est le véritable luxe et l'opulence de pacotille.

Dans une société de consommation comme celle de l'occident, où la majeure partie de la population a les moyens de satisfaire ses besoins primaires, les individus cherchent à se distinguer et à montrer leur supériorité. En effet, une personne recherche la particularité, la différence et l'exclusivité. Quel que soit l'objet, il peut être considéré comme un objet de luxe s'il est différent et s'il se distingue par sa grande qualité et sa perfection. Les yachts et les voiliers, les avions privés et les appareils électroniques dotés de la technologie la plus avancée, arrivent à être convoités par tous afin que chaque individu puisse marquer sa différence. Le luxe ne se traduit pas seulement par la possession physique d'un objet mais également par des expériences quotidiennes qui peuvent être, elles aussi, qualifiées de luxueuses.

Pour les cadres supérieurs qui ont un rythme de travail effréné, le luxe leur permet de profiter de leur temps libre avec leur famille ou leurs amis. Pour les amoureux de voitures, l'objet de luxe serait une rapide et puissante voiture de sport. Pour les personnes qui sont à la recherche d'émotions et en quête d'aventures, un impressionnant voilier pourrait les pousser à sillonner les mers du globe.

Dans ce livre ont été réunis des objets de luxe provenant de divers horizons. Sont présentés des voitures classiques, des modèles de sport, des motos, des yachts et des avions privés. Le lecteur peut également découvrir des destinations lointaines et profiter de petits objets exclusifs et déjà presque légendaires : tout a été réuni pour satisfaire les désirs des amoureux du luxe.

Luxury sailing

Navegación de lujo

Navigation de luxe

Luxury sailing
Navegación de lujo
Navigation de luxe

Navigating, whether in a powerful motorboat or in a speedy, stylish sailboat, is a fantastic experience that provokes a unique sensation of freedom and independence. These vessels provide an escape from day-to-day routines. They provide a means to visit idyllic places, remote islands, hidden coves... Navigating is associated with adventure, with holidays and of course, with luxury, opulence, and a life-style envied by many. This chapter exhibits elegant and fast sailboats with large, resistant sails that allow wind energy to be used. Although sailboats are traditionally associated with sport and adventure, they are not at odds with high quality and excellent manufacturing. The vessels shown here are fully-equipped and each detail has been added with great care. Thanks to their exceptionally powerful motors these yachts can be taken out to open sea at great speeds allowing the occupants to enjoy the sun far from the packed coastlines. They are also symbols of luxury, wealth and success and the rich and famous become even more desired and envied when they are spotted relaxing on their yachts. Over the next few pages, the most prestigious sailing and motorboat manufacturers have agreed to show us the best of their shipyards, their most exclusive and highest quality models, some of which are truly unique.

Navegar, ya sea en una potente embarcación de motor, ya sea en un veloz y estilizado velero, es una experiencia fantástica que provoca una singular sensación de libertad y de autonomía. Las embarcaciones nos alejan de nuestro mundo habitual y cotidiano, nos permiten escaparnos de nuestras rutinas y alejarnos hacia otros lugares más agradables, como recónditas islas o calas escondidas. Navegar se asocia a la aventura, a épocas estivales y vacacionales y, cómo no, se relaciona también con el lujo, con la opulencia y con un estilo de vida envidiable para muchos. En este capítulo se muestran elegantes y veloces veleros con grandes y resistentes velas que permiten utilizar la energía del viento. Los veleros se asocian al deporte y a la aventura, pero no están reñidos con la alta calidad y con una manufactura excelente. Las naves están equipadas con todas las comodidades y cada detalle se ha realizado con sumo esmero. Por otro lado, los yates son embarcaciones con motores especialmente potentes, que permiten separarse de la costa a gran velocidad para disfrutar del mar abierto y del sol. Son también símbolos de lujo, de riqueza, de éxito. Por ello, ricos y famosos son aún más deseados y envidiados cuando se encuentran disfrutando relajadamente de sus yates. Las más prestigiosas marcas de embarcaciones de vela y de motor muestran en las siguientes páginas lo mejor de sus astilleros, sus modelos más exclusivos y de mejor calidad, algunos de ellos embarcaciones únicas en el mundo.

Naviguer, que ce soit sur une puissante embarcation à moteur ou sur un voilier rapide et élégant, représente une expérience fantastique, qui provoque une extraordinaire sensation de liberté et d'autonomie. Ces embarcations nous mènent loin de notre quotidien et du monde habituel. Elles nous permettent d'échapper à la routine et de voyager vers d'autres destinations plus agréables comme les îles retirées ou les criques cachées. La navigation, associée à l'aventure, aux périodes estivales et aux vacances, fait incontestablement référence au luxe, à l'opulence et à un style de vie attrayant pour un grand nombre de personnes. Ce chapitre présente des voiliers rapides et élégants, dont les grandes voiles résistantes permettent d'utiliser l'énergie du vent. Les voiliers sont associés au sport et à l'aventure, mais ne sont pas incompatibles avec le haut de gamme et une construction d'excellente qualité. Ces navires parfaitement équipés offrent tout le confort nécessaire et chaque détail a été réalisé avec le plus grand soin. D'autre part, les yachts sont des embarcations à moteurs particulièrement puissants qui permettent de s'éloigner des côtes à grande vitesse afin de profiter de la haute mer et du soleil. Ils symbolisent également le luxe, la richesse et le succès. C'est pourquoi, les personnes riches et célèbres sont toujours plus jalousées lorsqu'elles profitent tranquillement de la vie à bord de leurs yachts. Les plus prestigieuses marques de bateaux à voile et à moteur présentent, dans les pages suivantes, le meilleur de leurs chantiers navals et leurs modèles les plus exclusifs. Certaines de ces embarcations sont uniques au monde.

LÜRSSEN Oasis

Oasis is Lürssen's second yacht with these characteristics, designed by Glade Johnson. It is a large yacht with elegant lines. The aim of the owners was to create a unique vessel, with an exclusive exterior design and a contemporary, cozy and luxurious interior. It has six very large cabins, an office and spectacular decks on the stern and bow. A large corridor with stairs on the main deck separates the private area from the main living room. There is an outdoor dining area on the stern deck that can be covered with a retractable canopy. A gym with glass doors separates the two outer decks. A lighting system and powerful music equipment can by used to convert the bow deck into a disco. The main living room is flooded with natural light through its huge windows. The kitchen and pantry are situated on the same deck, to make things easier for the occupants. The cabins are situated on the lower deck which allows their considerable dimensions. The helm, equipped with the latest technology, is on the upper deck.

Oasis es el segundo yate de Lürssen de estas características diseñado por Glade Johnson. Es un gran yate que mantiene unas líneas elegantes. El objetivo de los propietarios era crear una embarcación única, con un diseño exterior exclusivo y un interior contemporáneo, acogedor y lujoso. Cuenta con seis camarotes de grandes dimensiones, una oficina y unas espectaculares terrazas en la popa y en la proa. La cubierta principal ofrece un gran pasillo con unas escaleras que separan la zona privada del salón principal. En la terraza de popa se ha ubicado un comedor exterior que puede cubrirse con un toldo retráctil. Entre las dos terrazas se encuentra un gimnasio con puertas de cristal. La terraza de proa también se convierte en una discoteca gracias a un sistema de luces y a un potente equipo de música. El salón principal recibe gran cantidad de luz natural a través de unos grandes ventanales. Para proporcionar un mejor servicio a los ocupantes, la cocina y la despensa se encuentran en la misma cubierta. Los camarotes se sitúan en la cubierta inferior, lo que permite que tengan unas dimensiones notables. En la cubierta superior se encuentra la timonera, equipada con la última tecnología.

Oasis, dessiné par Glade Johnson, est le deuxième yacht construit par Luerssen dans cette catégorie et se distingue par ses lignes élégantes. L'objectif des propriétaires était de donner naissance à une embarcation unique, dotée d'un design extérieur exclusif et d'un intérieur moderne, accueillant et luxueux. Il est équipé de six cabines spacieuses, d'un bureau et d'impressionnantes terrasses, situées au niveau de la proue et de la poupe. Le pont principal offre un grand couloir avec des escaliers, qui séparent les parties communes du salon principal. Une salle à manger extérieure équipée d'un bimini rétractable a été aménagée sur la terrasse de la poupe du bateau. Sur les deux autres terrasses, un gymnase avec des portes en verre a été installé. La terrasse située à la proue peut être transformée en discothèque grâce à un système de lumières et à un puissant dispositif de sonorisation. Le salon principal est baigné par la lumière naturelle qui traverse les grandes baies vitrées. La cuisine et la réserve ont été aménagées sur le même pont afin d'offrir aux hôtes le meilleur service possible. Les cabines sont situées au niveau du pont inférieur, ainsi elles bénéficient toutes des mêmes dimensions. Dotée de la technologie la plus récente, la barre a été installée sur le pont supérieur.

TECHNICAL SPECIFICATIONS

Builder	Lürssen
Price	On request
Naval architecture	Lürssen
Design	Glade Johnson
Contact	www.luerssen.com
Engine	2 x Caterpillar 3,512 B, each 1,440 kW / 1,957 hp
Displacement	1,060 tons
Cruising speed	16 knots
Fuel capacity	39,617.19 gal	150,000 l
Water capacity	6,602.86 gal	25,000 l
Loa, beam, draft	178.48 ft	54.40 m, 37.47 ft	11.42 m, 11.48 ft	3.50 m
Classification	Lloyd's + 100 A1, SSC Yacht Mono G6, LMC, UMS full MCA compliance
Range	5,000 nm at 12 knots
Material	Steel hull and aluminum superstructure

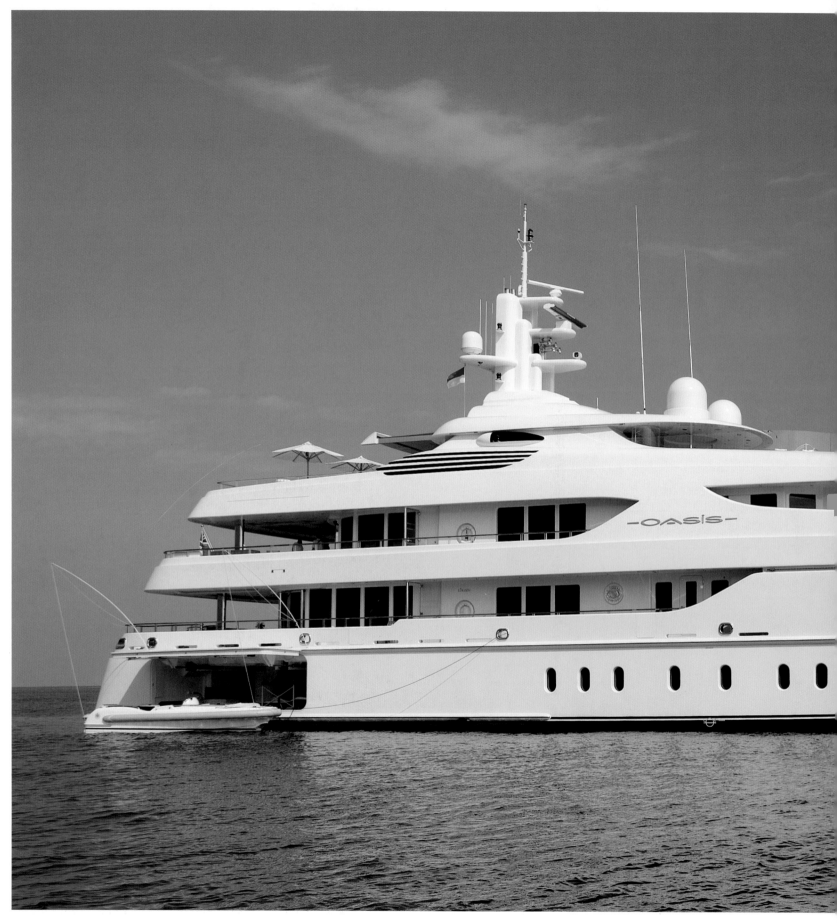

BENETTI AMNESIA

Originally commissioned by an English client, the Amnesia is a milestone in the evolution of Benetti as a manufacturer of luxury super yachts. The living room is the distinctive feature in the interior design of the Amnesia. Even the smallest details have been taken care of and the designers have managed to communicate it with the dining area. This originality of the layout, added to the differences in decoration from room to room, creates a special sensation of space that is uncommon in this kind of vessel. Two large seats are placed at an angle in the center of the living room, which can easily compare with any onshore mansion. The deck solarium can also be used as a helicopter landing pad, and the upper deck houses a Jacuzzi and a spacious leisure area ideal for cocktails.

Encargado a la firma por un cliente inglés, el Amnesia marca un hito en la trayectoria de Benetti como fabricante de superyates de lujo. El salón es el signo distintivo en el diseño de interiores del Amnesia, ya que en él se ha cuidado hasta el mínimo detalle y se ha conseguido incluso que comunique con el área del comedor. Esta distribución proporciona una sensación de amplitud completamente novedosa en este tipo de embarcaciones y, junto con la decoración de las diversas zonas del yate, confiere una atmósfera especial. Dos grandes asientos en ángulo se agrupan en el centro del salón, que no tiene nada que envidiar al de cualquier mansión de tierra firme. La cubierta solárium sirve también como pista de aterrizaje de helicópteros, mientras que la cubierta superior alberga un *jacuzzi* y una amplia zona de recreo ideal para tomar un cóctel.

Commandé par un client anglais, l'Amnesia marque un véritable tournant dans l'histoire de la construction des grands yachts de luxe chez Benetti. Le salon, qui communique avec la salle à manger et dans lequel les moindres détails ont été soignés, est le point fort du design intérieur de ce bateau. Sur ce type d'embarcation, cette distribution offre une impression d'espace complètement novatrice. Par ailleurs, la décoration des différentes zones confère à cet espace une atmosphère particulière. Deux grands sièges d'angle occupent le centre du salon qui n'a rien à envier à celui de n'importe quelle grande demeure située sur le continent. Le pont-solarium peut également servir de piste d'atterrissage pour hélicoptères, contrairement au pont supérieur qui a été aménagé pour accueillir un *jacuzzi* et une spacieuse aire de loisirs, idéale pour prendre un cocktail.

TECHNICAL SPECIFICATIONS

Builder	Benetti Shipyard
Price	On request
Naval architecture	Benetti Shipyard
Design	Stefano Natucci
Contact	www.benettiyachts.it
Engine	2 x Caterpillar 3,512
Displacement	680 tons
Top speed	16 knots
Fuel capacity	36,976.04 gal | 140,000 l
Water capacity	3,169.37 gal | 12,000 l
Loa, beam, draft	180.4 ft | 54.99 m, 33.45 ft | 10.20 m, 9.84 ft | 3 m
Classification	Lloyds register of shipping – MCA compliant
Range	5,000 nm approx.
Material	Steel hull and aluminum superstructure

LÜRSSEN LINDA LOU

This amazing yacht was delivered to the client in September 2006. The owner's original idea was to acquire a smaller vessel, but he changed his mind on seeing the Capri model and opted for a more spectacular design. Espen Oeino created a new design which took perfect advantage of the outer space. François Zuretti was commissioned with the interior design, which was to be classical and elegant. A corridor leads to the owner's room: a study and a bedroom with separate bathrooms and dressing rooms, for him and for her. A lounge area and a living room complete this area. The main living room is divided into various areas and is flooded with natural light thanks to its large windows. An extravagant marble bar separates it from the dining room. Another living room is located on the upper area, with different spaces for conversation and relaxing. The stern area can be converted into a disco. The captain's rooms and the gymnasium are beside the bridge that is equipped with the latest technology. This is most definitely an outstanding luxury yacht, perfecto for getting away from it all and enjoying well-deserved and luxurious holidays.

Este fantástico yate se entregó al cliente en septiembre de 2006. La idea inicial del propietario era la de adquirir una embarcación más pequeña, pero, al ver el modelo Capri, cambió de opinión y se decidió por un diseño más espectacular. Espen Oeino creó un nuevo diseño en el que el espacio exterior está perfectamente aprovechado. François Zuretti se encargó del diseño interior, que debía ser clásico y elegante. Un pasillo lleva a las dependencias del propietario, un estudio y un dormitorio con baños y vestidores separados, para él y para ella. Un área de *lounge* y una sala de estar completan esta zona. El salón principal, dividido en varias áreas, se inunda de luz natural gracias a las grandes ventanas, y un extravagante bar de mármol lo separa del comedor. En el área superior se ha ubicado otro salón, con diferentes espacios para conversar y relajarse. La zona de popa puede convertirse en discoteca; junto al puente de mando, que está equipado con la última tecnología, se encuentran las estancias del capitán y el gimnasio. En definitiva, se trata de un yate espectacular y lujoso, ideal para escaparse y disfrutar de unas merecidas y maravillosas vacaciones.

Ce fantastique yacht a été commandé par un client en septembre 2006. Au départ, celui-ci voulait acquérir une embarcation de très petite taille, mais en découvrant le modèle Capri, il changea d'avis, optant pour un design plus spectaculaire. Espen Oeino créa un nouveau design dans lequel l'espace extérieur est parfaitement optimisé. Le design intérieur, qui devait être classique et élégant, a été confié à François Zuretti. Un couloir mène aux pièces réservées au propriétaire, composées d'un bureau et d'une chambre à coucher avec salles de bains et vestiaires séparés, pour elle et pour lui. Un espace *lounge* et une salle de séjour complètent cette partie. Le salon principal, divisé en plusieurs zones, est inondé de lumière naturelle grâce aux grandes baies vitrées et est séparé de la salle à manger par un extravagant bar en marbre. Dans la partie supérieure, un autre salon, doté de différents espaces pour converser et se reposer, a été aménagé. La zone de la poupe du bateau peut être transformée en discothèque. Les quartiers réservés au capitaine et le gymnase se trouvent à côté de la passerelle de manœuvre équipée de la dernière technologie. En définitive, il s'agit d'un yacht spectaculaire et luxueux avec lequel il est possible de s'échapper pour profiter de merveilleuses vacances bien méritées.

TECHNICAL SPECIFICATIONS

Builder	Lürssen
Price	On request
Naval architecture	Lürssen
Design	François Zuretti (interior), Espen Oeino (exterior)
Contact	www.luerssen.com
Engine	2 x Caterpillar 3,512 B, each 1,440 kW / 1,957 hp
Displacement	1,070 tons
Cruising speed	15.5 knots
Fuel capacity	39,617.19 gal | 150,000 l
Water capacity	7,395.21 gal | 28,000 l
Loa, beam, draft	196.85 ft | 60 m, 37.63 ft | 11.47 m, 11.48 ft | 3.50 m
Classification	Lloyd's LR + 100 A1, SSC Yacht Mono G6, LMC, UMS full MCA compliance
Range	5,000 nm at 12 knots
Material	Steel hull and aluminum superstructure

ASTONDOA 122 GLX

This magnificent, nearly 125 ft-long yacht, is one of the latest creations of Astondoa. The straight, polished lines of the hull reflect the essence of the second vessel in the GLX range. The high water line and the prominent bow further accentuate the yacht's magnificent aesthetics. The design of the exterior, commissioned to Astondoa, has prioritized comfort and safety over large open spaces. The wide corridors, the railings and the ease of passage between the bathing platform and the transom are examples of this fundamentally practical concept that does not cut back on elegance and quality. The outdoor decks provide spaces for relaxing. The bow structure has a solarium with capacity for three people and a refreshing jacuzzi has been installed on the flying bridge. An outdoor eating area to seat twelve people is located beside this. All the spaces can be personalized and decorated according to each client's ideas, whether in the kitchen, the cabins or the living rooms, etc.

Este magnífico yate, de casi 38 m de eslora, es una de las últimas creaciones de Astondoa. Las líneas rectas y depuradas del casco son la mejor presentación para esta segunda embarcación de la gama GLX. El franco bordo, que está situado a una gran altura, y el lanzamiento de proa contribuyen a acentuar la magnífica estética del yate. El diseño del exterior, a cargo de Astondoa, ha priorizado la comodidad y la seguridad sobre los grandes espacios abiertos. Los amplios pasillos, los pasamanos y la facilidad de paso entre la plataforma de baño y la bañera son ejemplos de este concepto basado en lo práctico, pero que no olvida la elegancia y la calidad. Los exteriores proporcionan espacios para el relax. En la estructura de proa, por ejemplo, se ha situado un solárium con capacidad para tres personas y en el *flying bridge* se ha instalado un refrescante *jacuzzi*. Junto a él, se encuentra un comedor exterior para 12 comensales. Éstos y todos los demás espacios interiores pueden personalizarse de acuerdo con las ideas y preferencias de cada cliente con respecto a la decoración, ya sea de la cocina, los camarotes, los salones, etc.

Ce magnifique yacht –de près de 38 mètres de long–, est l'une des dernières créations d'Astondoa. Les lignes droites et soignées de la coque sont les meilleurs atouts pour ce deuxième bateau de la gamme GLX. Le niveau élevé de la ligne de flottaison ainsi que l'avancée de la proue contribuent à souligner son esthétique. Le design extérieur, réalisé par Astondoa, a privilégié le confort et la sécurité au niveau des grands espaces ouverts. Les couloirs spacieux, les lignes de vie et les facilités de passage entre la plateforme de bain et la jupe du bateau illustrent parfaitement ce concept basé sur l'utilisation fonctionnelle des espaces, sans oublier l'élégance et la qualité. Les extérieurs offrent des zones de repos. Par exemple, un solarium pour trois personnes a été installé à la proue du bateau et sur le *flying bridge*, un rafraîchissant jacuzzi a été aménagé. À côté de ce jacuzzi, se trouve une salle à manger extérieure pouvant accueillir douze convives. Tous ces espaces ainsi que les pièces intérieures peuvent être personnalisés en fonction des idées et des préférences de chaque client qui peuvent choisir la décoration de la cuisine, des cabines, des salons, etc.

TECHNICAL SPECIFICATIONS

Builder	Astilleros Astondoa
Price	On request
Naval architecture	Astondoa
Design	Astondoa
Contact	www.astondoa.es
Engine	3 x MTU V16 M91
Displacement	155.29 tons
Cruising speed	24 knots
Fuel capacity	6,338.75 gal	24.000 l
Water capacity	1,373.40 gal	5.200 l
Loa, beam, draft	122.70 ft	37,40 m, 24.93 ft	7,60 m, 6.23 ft	1,90 m
Classification	N.I.
Range	N.I.
Material	N.I.

RIVA 115' ATHENA

Although the design and configuration of the boat cannot be altered, the interior of these spectacular 115 ft yachts can be, to a great extent, adapted to the client's specific needs, with first-class advice and guarantees provided by the prestigious Officina Italiana Design. Thus, they will have the option of fitting out another 4 or 5 cabins apart from the main one. Exquisite attention to detail in the choice of wood and upholstery has produced interiors of incomparable elegance, with an atmosphere in the very best 'lounge' tradition, while, at the same time, the design also guarantees that the occupants are comfortable, offering features such as a jacuzzi and a lounge with a 360-degree panoramic view and the capacity to accommodate up to ten people. The glass strip running all the way round the yacht provides perfect natural lighting for the various areas inside the yacht. With a maximum speed of 27 knots, to date only five boats have been built for this model, which continues the excellent work associated with the Italian firm of Riva.

Aunque el diseño y la configuración de la embarcación sean invariables, cada comprador de este espectacular yate de 35 m de eslora podrá personalizar gran parte de los espacios interiores según sus necesidades, contando con el asesoramiento y la garantía de calidad de la prestigiosa Officina Italiana Design. De esta manera, podrá escoger entre habilitar cuatro o cinco camarotes además del principal. Una atención exquisita a los detalles de la madera y las tapicerías empleadas ha dado como resultado unos interiores de elegancia inigualable, con un ambiente *lounge*. Al mismo tiempo, el diseño ofrece comodidad a sus ocupantes con prestaciones como una bañera *jacuzzi* y un salón con vistas panorámicas de 360° y capacidad para 10 personas. La franja acristalada que recorre todo el largo del yate permite una correcta iluminación de los interiores con luz natural. Con una velocidad máxima de 27 nudos, por el momento tan sólo se han construido cinco barcos de este modelo, que continúa con la línea de excelencia asociada a la firma italiana Riva.

Même si le design et la configuration de l'embarcation ne peuvent être modifiés, tout acheteur de ce yacht spectaculaire de 35 m de long pourra personnaliser une grande partie des espaces intérieurs en fonction de ses besoins, comptant sur les conseils et la garantie de qualité de la prestigieuse Officina Italiana Design. Ainsi, il pourra décider d'aménager quatre ou cinq cabines en plus de la cabine principale. Une attention toute particulière a été portée aux détails des boiseries et des tissus, permettant d'obtenir des intérieurs d'une élégance inégalable dans une ambiance très *lounge*. Le design assure à la fois le confort des occupants, des prestations telles qu'une baignoire jacuzzi, un salon avec vue panoramique et une capacité d'accueil de dix personnes. La baie vitrée parcourant la longueur du yacht permet un bon éclairage des intérieurs grâce à la lumière naturelle. Le yacht atteint une vitesse maximale de 27 nœuds. Jusqu'à présent, seulement cinq bateaux de ce modèle ont été construits, et celui-ci assure la continuité de l'excellence associée à la firme italienne Riva.

TECHNICAL SPECIFICATIONS

Builder	Riva, Italy
Price	On request
Naval architecture	Riva Engineering Department
Design	Officina Italiana Design
Contact	www.riva-yacht.com
Engine	2 x MTU 12V 4,000 M90, 2,775 Mhp
Displacement	156 tons
Cruising speed	23 knots
Fuel capacity	6,246.31 gal	23,650 l
Water capacity	845.17 gal	3,200 l
Loa, beam, draft	115 ft	35 m, 23.23 ft	7.08 m, 6.73 ft	2.05 m
Classification	CE design category 2003/44
Range	680 nm
Material	Fiberglass (exterior), wood (interiors)

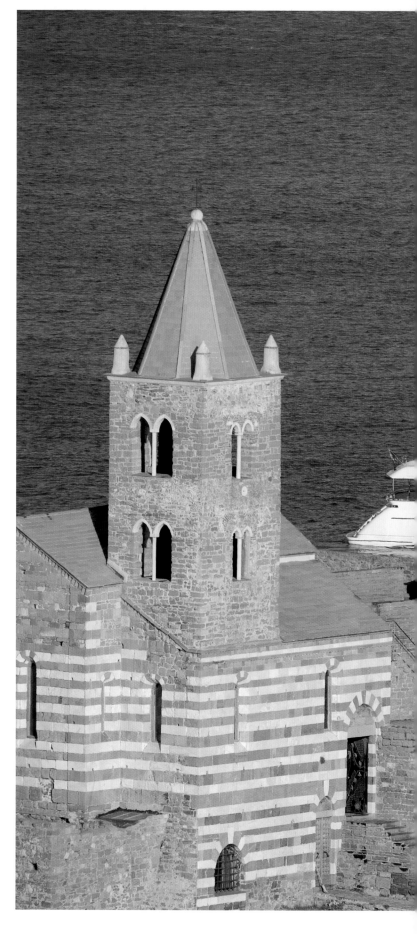

AICON 85 FLY

The new insignia ship of Aicon, the Aicon 85 Fly, is a sporting vessel, with an elegant design and a unique style. The interior-exterior design of the yacht has been studied carefully in order to optimize the space and thereby guarantee maximum comfort and a luxurious ambience. The bridge, which provides exceptional views, the dining room with a fully-equipped kitchen, the luxurious cabins and the large portholes make this vessel unique. The latest technology is complemented by a taste for detail and perfect finishes. A spacious stern deck can be used for sunbathing. The bridge has an area with sofas and a minibar create an ideal atmosphere for chatting under the elements. In the interior, all four comfortable cabins have high ceilings, luxurious finishes and a private bathroom. The owner's cabin is located in the aft and has its own desk, dressing table and dressing room. Fully-equipped and not lacking in details for an unforgettable time on board.

El nuevo buque insignia de Aicon, el Aicon 85 Fly, es una embarcación deportiva, con un diseño elegante y un estilo único. El interior y el exterior del yate se han estudiado con atención para optimizar el aprovechamiento del espacio y garantizar así el máximo confort y un ambiente lujoso. El puente de mando, que proporciona unas excepcionales vistas, el comedor, que cuenta con una cocina equipada, los lujosos camarotes y los grandes ojos de buey hacen de esta embarcación una pieza única. La última tecnología se complementa con el gusto por el detalle y con unos acabados perfectos. Una amplia cubierta de popa permite disfrutar de baños de sol. En el puente de mando, una zona de sofás y un minibar crean el ambiente ideal para disfrutar de una agradable conversación al abrigo del viento y del sol. En el interior, cada uno de los cuatro confortables camarotes cuenta con altos techos, lujosos acabados y baño propio. El camarote del propietario, situado en la popa, posee su propio escritorio, tocador y vestidor. Todos los detalles y las comodidades para una inolvidable estancia a bordo.

Le nouveau fleuron d'Aicon, l'Aicon 85 Fly, est une embarcation sportive dotée d'un design élégant et d'un style unique. Le design intérieur et extérieur du yacht a été minutieusement étudié pour optimiser l'utilisation de l'espace et garantir un environnement luxueux et le maximum de confort. La passerelle de manœuvre qui offre une vue exceptionnelle, la salle à manger dotée d'une cuisine équipée, ainsi que les luxueuses cabines et les grands hublots, font de cette embarcation un modèle unique. Le goût du détail et les finitions parfaites complètent la technologie la plus récente. Le pont spacieux, situé au niveau de la poupe, permet de prendre des bains de soleil. Sur la passerelle de manœuvre, des canapés et un minibar créent l'environnement idéal pour converser à l'abri du vent et du soleil. A l'intérieur, chacune des quatre confortables cabines est dotée de hauts plafonds, de luxueuses finitions et d'une salle de bain privée. La cabine du propriétaire, située à la poupe du bateau, est dotée d'un bureau et possède un cabinet de toilette et un dressing. Tout est prévu pour que le séjour à bord reste inoubliable.

TECHNICAL SPECIFICATIONS

Builder	Aicon
Price	€ 4,150,000 (indicative price)
Naval architecture	Aicon Yachts
Design	Marco Mannino
Contact	www.aiconyachts.com
Engine	2 x Caterpillar C32 Acert – 2 x 1,825 bhp
Displacement	75 tons
Cruising speed	27 knots
Fuel capacity	1,875.21 gal	7,100 l
Water capacity	528.23 gal	2,000 l
Loa, beam, draft	85.83 ft	26.16 m, 21.06 ft	6.42 m, 3.61 ft	1.10 m
Classification	A
Range	5,000 nm at 12 knots
Material	Steel hull and aluminum superstructure

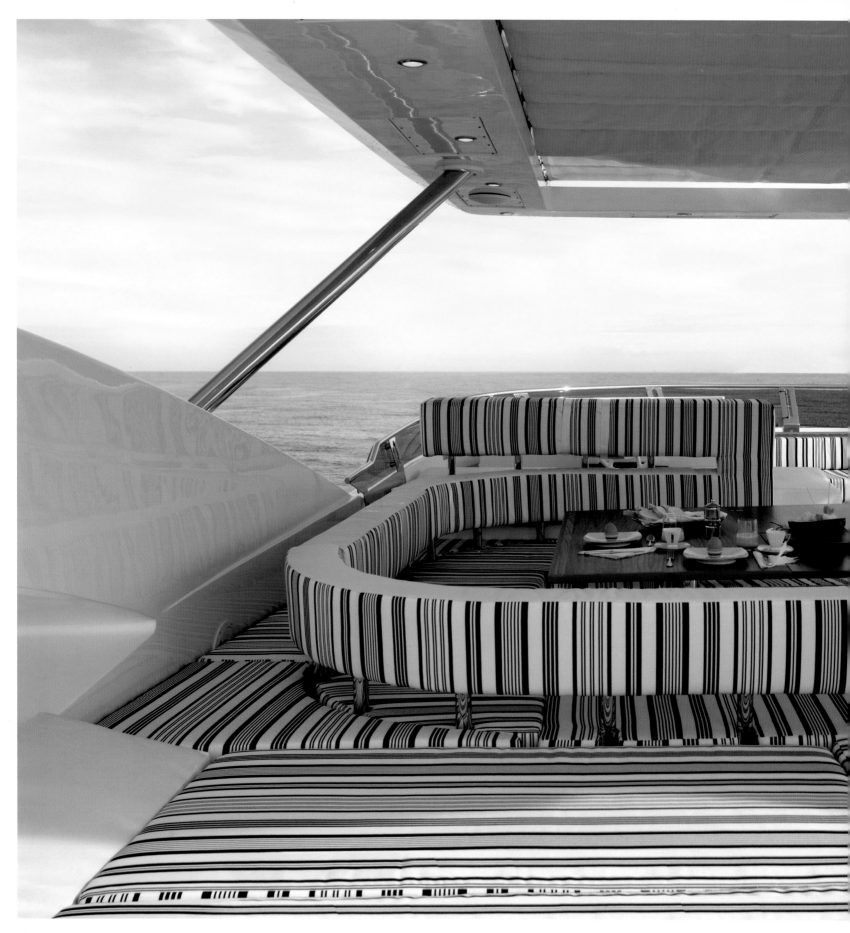

WALLY 143 ESENSE

The design of this great sailboat with a total length of 143 ft, originally commissioned from Wally by a private European citizen, brings together elements that are noticeably retro in spirit and details that are decidedly contemporary in style. The large gunwale, guaranteeing safety and privacy on deck, is not at all conventional for this type of boat, but actually derives its inspiration from the gunwales of certain classical vessels. The deck is unusually bare, and lacking in any areas that have been marked off for specific purposes. This clarity of design turns the deck into a space measuring 1,938 ft² with comfort and flexibility being its most striking characteristics. The stern has a "terrace over the sea", an area of 226 ft² which is connected to a large indoor lounge that can be extended if the cabins for the guests are included. The hull is dark gray with a metallic finish, whereas inside there is a predominance of white and paduk wood. The raised keel reduces the boat's draft from 10 to 13 ft, enabling it to navigate in shallow waters. Thanks to its attractive design and the absence of any superfluous elements, the vessel is reminiscent of a giant version of a boat in the America's Cup.

El diseño de este gran velero de 43 m de eslora, encargado originalmente a Wally por un particular europeo, reúne elementos de un marcado espíritu retro con detalles de estilo decididamente contemporáneo. La gruesa borda, que garantiza la seguridad y la privacidad en la cubierta, resulta poco convencional en este tipo de embarcaciones, pero en realidad se inspira en las bordas de algunas naves clásicas. La cubierta está insólitamente despejada, sin que se demarquen zonas específicas. Esta ausencia de elementos convierte la cubierta en un espacio de 180 m² cuyas características más destacadas son la comodidad y la flexibilidad. La popa cuenta con una "terraza sobre el mar", un espacio de 21 m² que conecta con el gran salón interior y que puede prolongarse al incorporar los camarotes para invitados. El casco es de un gris oscuro con acabado metálico, mientras que en los interiores priman los acabados en blanco y en madera de paduk. La quilla elevada reduce el calado de 6 a 4 m, lo cual permite la navegación en aguas poco profundas. Por su atractivo diseño y por la ausencia de elementos superfluos, la embarcación recuerda a un barco de la Copa América en versión gigante.

Le design de ce grand voilier de 43 m de long, commandé à l'origine à Wally par un particulier européen, associe des éléments rétro marquants et des détails résolument contemporains. Le bord épais, qui garantit sécurité et intimité sur le pont, est peu conventionnel sur ce type d'embarcations mais s'inspire en réalité de certains navires classiques. Le pont est singulièrement dégagé, sans qu'aucune zone spécifique ne se démarque. Cette pureté d'éléments le transforme en un espace de 180 m² dont les principales caractéristiques sont le confort et la polyvalence. La poupe dispose d'une « terrasse sur la mer » de 21 m² qui rejoint le grand salon intérieur et qui peut être prolongée si l'on y incorpore les cabines pour les invités. La coque est d'un gris foncé métallisé, alors qu'à l'intérieur les finitions blanches et en bois padouk dominent. La quille élevée réduit le tirant d'eau de 6 à 4 m, ce qui permet une navigation en eaux peu profondes. Grâce à son design séduisant et à l'absence d'éléments superflus, l'embarcation rappelle un bateau de l'America's Cup en version géante.

TECHNICAL SPECIFICATIONS

Builder	Wally
Price	€ 20,000,000
Naval architecture	Wally, Tripp Design
Design	Wally, Odile Decq
Contact	www.wally.com
Type	Fast Cruising Sloop
Loa, beam, draft	143.37 ft | 43.7 m, 28.12 ft | 8.57 m, 13-19.69 ft | 4-6 m
Sail area	9,687 ft² | 900 m²
Engine	Caterpillar 550 hp 2,100 rpm
Displacement	140 tons
Top speed	14 knots
Fuel capacity	3,697.60 gal | 14,000 l Paduk wood, carbon fiber
Material	

WALLY 80 TANGO

The goal of the creators of this model from the firm Wally —Farr Yacht Design for the lines of the hull, Lazzarini Pickering Architects for the interior design— was to come up with a competitive sailboat that would guarantee the presence of spacious areas inside the vessel. A beam of nearly 20 ft means that the vessel can be fitted out with a generous lounge that can hold up to 10 people at the same time. Since it is wider than other 80 ft vessels, the Tango is also more stable and roomy, and therefore it is easier to sail and does not require such a large crew. A skylight occupying the central part of the deck fills the interior with light, which reflects Wally's determination to look for the ultimate way to connect the exterior with the interior of their vessels. For optimum use, the deck is divided into three areas: one which can be covered with cushions and used for meetings the pilotage cabin and the sun deck. The pilotage cabin is also larger than usual and has two folding tables that can accommodate 10 people for a meal.

El objetivo conjunto de los creadores de este modelo de la firma Wally —Farr Yacht Design para las líneas del casco y Lazzarini Pickering Architects para el diseño de interiores— era el de conseguir un velero competitivo que ofreciera unos interiores espaciosos. Una manga de casi 6 m permite la habilitación de un amplio salón que puede acoger a un máximo de diez personas. Al ser más ancho que otras naves de 24 m, el Tango también es más espacioso y estable, de modo que su tripulación resulta más sencilla. Una claraboya, que ocupa la parte central de la cubierta, inunda los interiores de luz y redunda en el empeño de Wally de comunicar, en la medida de lo posible, el exterior con el interior de las embarcaciones. Para optimizar su uso, la cubierta se divide en tres espacios: uno que puede cubrirse con cojines y se emplea como zona de reunión, la cabina de pilotaje y el solárium. La cabina de pilotaje también es mayor de lo habitual y cuenta con dos mesas plegables a las que se pueden sentar diez personas.

L'objectif commun des créateurs de ce modèle de la firme Wally (Farr Yacht Design pour les lignes de la coque, Lazzarini Pickering Architects pour la conception des intérieurs) était d'obtenir un voilier compétitif garantissant des intérieurs spacieux. Une largeur de presque 6 m permet d'aménager un vaste salon pouvant accueillir jusqu'à dix personnes. Étant plus large que d'autres embarcations de 24 m, le Tango est aussi plus spacieux et plus stable, permettant une navigation plus facile et requérant moins de personnel navigant. Une lucarne qui occupe la partie centrale du pont baigne les intérieurs de lumière et correspond au désir de Wally de faire communiquer, dans la mesure du possible, l'extérieur et l'intérieur des embarcations. Pour optimiser son usage, le pont se divise en trois espaces : un qui peut être décoré de coussins, servant de zone de réunion, la cabine de pilotage et le solarium. La cabine de pilotage est plus grande qu'à l'accoutumée et dispose de deux tables pliantes autour desquelles peuvent s'asseoir dix personnes pour prendre un repas.

TECHNICAL SPECIFICATIONS

Builder	Wally
Price	€ 4,950,000
Naval architecture	Wally, Farr Yacht Design
Design	Wally, Lazzarini Pickering Architects
Contact	www.wally.com
Type	Fast cruising sloop
Loa, beam, draft	78.71 ft | 24 m, 19.55 ft | 5.96 m, 13.12 ft | 4 m
Sail area	3,455.22 ft² | 321 m²
Engine	Yanmar 190 hp
Displacement	35 tons
Top speed	10 knots
Fuel capacity	528.23 gal | 2,000 l
Material	Carbon fiber, aluminum, titanium, teak

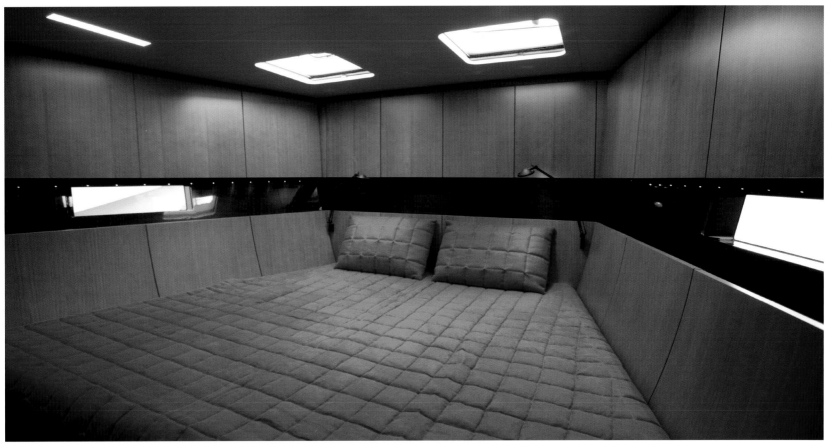

NAUTOR'S SWAN   SWAN 131

This yacht is the longest model commercialized by the company which was founded in 1966 by the Finn Pekka Koskenkylä. It was created in June 2006 and is the new insignia ship of the Nautor's Swan factory. The vessel combines style with impressive dimensions and great resistance. All this has been made possible by the Frers team, whose experience means they are accustomed to blending beauty with advanced technology in the boat designs they are commissioned. It is a majestic sailboat of considerable size (131,23 ft long) with a 27.8 ft beam, a deck area for two rudders, and a large leisure area. Moreover, its spacious deck can be put to many uses, and guarantees spacious and comfortable interiors. The living-dining room, decorated by the talented Dick Young, could easily be confused with the interior of a luxurious city apartment. This is also true for the cabins, where the elegant wood finishes are very impressive.

Este modelo es el yate de mayor eslora de los que comercializa la marca fundada en 1966 por el finlandés Pekka Koskenkylä. Nacido en junio de 2006, se trata del nuevo buque insignia de Nautor's Swan. Esta embarcación conjuga su estilo con sus impresionantes dimensiones y su resistencia. Esto ha sido posible gracias a la experiencia del equipo Frers, acostumbrado a aunar belleza y alta tecnología en los diseños de los barcos que realiza. Sus 40 m de eslora y casi 9 de manga lo convierten en un majestuoso velero de gran tamaño, con espacio en cubierta para dos timones y una amplia zona de recreo. Además, su enorme cubierta permite muy distintos usos y configuraciones, y ofrece unos interiores espaciosos y confortables. Gracias al talento del decorador Dick Young, el salón comedor no tiene nada que envidiar al de cualquier apartamento de lujo, ni tampoco los camarotes, donde la elegancia de los revestimientos de madera no deja de impresionar.

Ce modèle est le plus long yacht commercialisé par la marque fondée en 1966 par le Finlandais Pekka Koskenkylä. Nouveau fleuron des chantiers Nautor's Swan, il est né en juin 2006 et conjugue dimensions impressionnantes, résistance et élégance. Sa conception a été possible grâce à l'expérience de l'équipe Frers, habituée à allier beauté et haute technologie dans la construction de ses bateaux. Quarante mètres de long et près de neuf mètres de large font de cette embarcation un majestueux voilier. Il est doté d'un espace couvert pouvant accueillir deux gouvernails et d'une spacieuse aire de loisirs. Par ailleurs, son vaste pont permet différentes utilisations et configurations, et garantit des intérieurs spacieux et confortables à la fois. Grâce aux talents du décorateur Dick Young, le salon-salle à manger et les cabines, où l'élégance des revêtements en bois ne cesse d'impressionner, n'ont rien à envier à n'importe quel appartement de luxe.

TECHNICAL SPECIFICATIONS

Builder	Nautor's Swan Custom
Price	On request
Naval architecture	German Frers
Design	Dick Young
Contact	www.nautorswan.com
Type	Custom Yacht
Loa, beam, draft	131.23 ft | 40 m, 27.8 ft | 8.50 m, 15.75 ft | 4.80 m
Sail area	Fore triangle 4,021.61 ft² | 373.62 m²; main sail 3,956.17 ft² | 367.54 m²
Engine	2 x 490 Bhp
Displacement	200 tons
Top speed	14 knots
Fuel capacity	3,433.49 gal | 13,000 l
Material	Composite, sandwich

WALLY 70 WALLYPOWER

The 70 WallyPower project, a powerful launch, has successfully integrated an innovative design and the latest technology to create a fast, comfortable, safe and stylish vessel. Its features make it ideal for enjoying the outdoor decks, and the lines of its hull, stylized and dynamic, provide an elegant and modern aesthetic. A crystal structure, with special filters against the sun's rays and heat, protects the inside of the yacht. The living room, located below this structure, is especially spacious and large, and eight people can be seated comfortably in the dining room. There is another elegant sitting and eating area on the stern. Moreover, the 70 WallyPower is the safest launch of its kind, thanks to the unique design of the bow deck. Three different versions of this vessel exist, with varieties in the distribution of the indoor spaces and the capacity. The main bedroom of the Suite version occupies two thirds of the indoor space. It also has a cabin for the crew.

El proyecto de la 70 WallyPower, una potente lancha, ha conseguido integrar un diseño innovador y la última tecnología para crear una embarcación rápida, confortable, segura y con estilo. Sus características la hacen apropiada para disfrutar del exterior, y sus líneas del casco, estilizadas y dinámicas, proporcionan una estética elegante y moderna. Resguarda el interior del yate una estructura de cristal que incorpora filtros especiales para proteger de los rayos solares y del calor. El salón, ubicado bajo esta estructura, es especialmente amplio y grande; en el comedor interior pueden sentarse confortablemente ocho comensales. En la popa, se encuentra otra elegante área para sentarse y comer. Además, y gracias a su particular diseño de la cubierta de proa, la 70 WallyPower es la lancha más segura de su clase. Existen tres versiones diferentes de esta embarcación, que cambian tanto la distribución de los espacios interiores como la capacidad de la lancha. La versión Suite, por ejemplo, está dotada de un dormitorio principal, que ocupa dos tercios del espacio interior, y de un camarote para la tripulación.

Le projet de la WallyPower 70, une puissante chaloupe, a réussi à associer un design novateur aux dernières technologies pour concevoir une embarcation rapide, confortable, sûre et élégante. Ses caractéristiques invitent avant tout à profiter de l'extérieur et les lignes stylisées et dynamiques de sa coque offrent une esthétique agréable et moderne à l'ensemble. Une structure en verre, dotée de filtres spéciaux contre les rayons du soleil et la chaleur, protège l'intérieur du yacht. Le salon, situé sous cette structure, est particulièrement spacieux et la salle à manger intérieure peut accueillir confortablement huit convives. Un autre espace pour se détendre et prendre les repas a été aménagé sur la poupe. Par ailleurs, et grâce au design particulier de la proue, la WallyPower 70 est la chaloupe la plus sûre de sa catégorie. Trois versions différentes de cette embarcation sont disponibles sur le marché. Les modifications portent sur la distribution des espaces intérieurs et sur la capacité de la chaloupe. La version Suite, par exemple, est équipée d'une chambre à coucher principale, qui occupe les deux tiers de l'espace intérieur, et d'une cabine réservée à l'équipage.

TECHNICAL SPECIFICATIONS

Builder	WallyEurope, Italy
Price	€ 3,200,000
Naval architecture	Wally-Allseas
Design	Wally, Gillian Brown
Contact	www.wally.com
Engine	2 x MTU 10V 2000 M93 (propulsion system)
Displacement	34 tons
Cruising speed	40 knots (max. speed)
Fuel capacity	2 x 1,003.64 gal | 2 x 3,800 l
Water capacity	171.67 gal | 650 l
Loa, beam, draft	71.85 ft | 21.90 m, 17.98 ft | 5.48 m, 3.08 ft | 0.94 m
Classification	CE Design category A
Range	300 nm (at max speed)
Material	Carbon fiber, teak

WALLY WallyTender

The WallyTender launch is the quintessence of the pleasure of navigation, of speed, of enjoying the sea and the open air. This vessel is a light construction with an advanced hull design that sails smoothly at any speed and in all weather conditions. The design of the interior has created a comfortable space and applied practical solutions to all the construction details, such as the handcrafted carbon fiber structured chairs. The made-to-order components define the Wally methodology of combining functional design with style. The exterior combines safety and comfort; it has padded seats, double sun loungers and a spacious deck. The model has been made in two versions, the Day Cruiser and the Overnight Cruiser. Both versions have a fully-equipped bathroom; the Overnight model also has a small cabin located under the forward deck. It is, in fact, a perfect launch for enjoying moments of genuine luxury.

La lancha WallyTender es la expresión física del placer de la navegación, de la velocidad, del mar y del aire libre. Esta embarcación combina una construcción ligera con el diseño avanzado de su casco, que consiguen una navegación suave a cualquier velocidad y en todas las condiciones meteorológicas. El diseño del interior crea un espacio confortable, con soluciones prácticas que se han aplicado a cada detalle de la construcción, como los asientos de estructura de fibra de carbono, hechos a mano. Los componentes realizados a medida definen la metodología de Wally para unir diseño funcional y estilo. El exterior combina seguridad y comodidad; ofrece asientos acolchados, tumbonas dobles y un amplio espacio de cubierta. El modelo se ha hecho en dos versiones, la Day Cruiser y la Overnight Cruiser. Ambas embarcaciones están totalmente equipadas con un baño completo; el modelo Overnight tiene además un pequeño camarote situado bajo la cubierta de proa. Se trata, en definitiva, de la lancha perfecta para disfrutar de momentos de auténtico lujo.

La chaloupe WallyTender est la quintessence du plaisir de naviguer, d'être rapide et permet de profiter pleinement de la mer et du grand air. La construction légère de cette embarcation est associée au design moderne de sa coque. Ainsi, quelle que soit la vitesse et les conditions météorologiques, la navigation est toujours très agréable. Le design intérieur crée un espace confortable offrant des solutions fonctionnelles qui ont été appliquées à chaque détail de la construction, comme les sièges en fibre de carbone fabriqués de manière artisanale. Les composants fabriqués sur mesure caractérisent la technique utilisée par Wally pour conjuguer design fonctionnel et élégance. L'extérieur combine sécurité et confort et offre à ses hôtes des sièges matelassés, des double-transats et un pont spacieux. Le modèle est disponible en deux versions : Day Cruiser et Overnight Cruiser. Les deux embarcations sont totalement équipées et dotées d'une salle de bain complète. De plus, le modèle Overnight offre une petite cabine supplémentaire, située sous le pont de la proue. Il s'agit, en définitive, de la chaloupe idéale pour profiter de purs instants de luxe.

TECHNICAL SPECIFICATIONS

Builder	WallyEurope, Italy
Price	€ 510,000
Naval architecture	Wally, Allseas
Design	Wally, Allseas
Contact	www.wally.com
Engine	2 x Cummins-Mercruiser D4.2L 320 hp
Displacement	5.8 t (Day Cruiser)
Cruising speed	30 knots
Fuel capacity	2 x 253.55 gal	2 x 960 l
Water capacity	63.39 gal	240 l
Loa, beam, draft	44.62 ft	13.60 m, 14.11 ft	4.30 m, 1.97 ft	0.60 m
Classification	CE Design category A
Range	400 nm (at cruising speed)
Material	Sandwich of fiberglass and carbon fiber

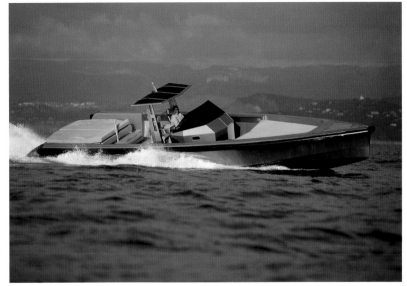

Luxury driving

Conducción de lujo

Conduite de luxe

Luxury driving
Conducción de lujo
Conduite de luxe

Driving is synonymous with luxury for many people. The sensation of controlling a vehicle while traveling miles and miles along desert roads or while contemplating different landscapes is a very pleasurable experience. For independent-minded people, driving is all about personal enjoyment of small moments in time. And emotions are multiplied a thousand-fold if the car or motorcycle being driven is a luxury range vehicle. Besides the innovative mechanics, these vehicles drive superbly, are extremely safe, and have endless options for personalization. They are often manufactured with great craftsmanship. The materials used such as teak wood, steel or leather, are chosen for their quality and then manipulated to obtain excellent results. The combination of all these elements results in enviable machines, of great precision and power, that are years ahead of conventional vehicles. Luxurious models with a wealth of details have been included in the following pages; elegant, powerful and exclusive vehicles that are objects of desire and symbols of status, excellence and luxury. BMW, Mercedes-Benz, Jaguar, Lamborghini, Ferrari and many other manufacturers exhibit their most lavish and perfect models here. Be careful, the adrenalin rush from driving one of these incredible machines can cause addiction.

La conducción es para muchas personas un verdadero lujo. La sensación de controlar los vehículos, recorrer kilómetros y kilómetros por carreteras desiertas y contemplar el paisaje les proporciona un auténtico placer. Para aquellos que valoran la independencia, conducir es disfrutar del tiempo y de pequeños momentos para sí mismos. Si, además, el coche o la motocicleta que se conduce es un vehículo de alta gama y de gran lujo, las emociones se multiplican por mil. Además de ser vehículos con una mecánica extraordinaria e innovadora, las prestaciones en cuanto a conducción y seguridad son inmensas y los detalles que se pueden personalizar parecen no acabarse nunca. Su fabricación es en ocasiones casi artesanal y los materiales utilizados, como la madera de teca, el acero o la piel, han sido escogidos por su calidad y manipulados para alcanzar unos resultados inmejorables. La combinación de todos estos elementos redunda en unas máquinas envidiables, de gran precisión y potencia, que están a años luz de las prestaciones de los utilitarios convencionales. En las siguientes páginas se han incluido modelos lujosos, muy ricos en detalles; vehículos extremadamente elegantes, potentes y exclusivos que demuestran la razón por la que todos ellos son objetos de deseo y símbolos de alto estatus, de excelencia y de lujo. BMW, Mercedes-Benz, Jaguar, Lamborghini, Ferrari y muchos más fabricantes exhiben aquí sus modelos más fastuosos y perfectos. Atención, la sensación de goce y deleite que se experimenta al conducir una de estas increíbles máquinas puede provocar adicción.

Pour bien des gens, conduire est un véritable luxe. Maîtriser un véhicule, parcourir des kilomètres et des kilomètres sur des routes désertes et contempler le paysage, leur procure un authentique plaisir. Pour les personnes qui apprécient l'indépendance, conduire permet de profiter d'agréables moments en toute tranquillité. Et si elles conduisent une voiture ou une moto haut de gamme, les émotions sont multipliées par mille. Ces véhicules ne sont pas seulement dotés d'une mécanique extraordinaire et novatrice, leurs prestations en ce qui concerne la conduite et la sécurité sont prodigieuses et les détails qui peuvent les personnaliser semblent infinis. Pour certains modèles, la fabrication est presque artisanale. Les matériaux utilisés, comme le teck, l'acier ou le cuir, choisis pour leur qualité, ont été travaillés pour obtenir des résultats exceptionnels. La combinaison de tous ces éléments génère des voitures fascinantes de précision et de puissance. Il faut dire que leurs prestations sont à des années lumières de celles des voitures traditionnelles. Dans les pages suivantes, des modèles de luxe sont décrits avec une grande précision. Ces véhicules, extrêmement élégants et puissants, sont présentés en exclusivité et montrent pourquoi ils sont des objets de désir et le symbole de la réussite sociale, de l'excellence et du luxe. BMW, Mercedes-Benz, Jaguar, Lamborghini, Ferrari et beaucoup d'autres constructeurs exposent ici leurs modèles les plus luxueux et les plus réussis. Attention, le plaisir et la volupté ressentis en conduisant une de ces incroyables machines peut provoquer une dépendance.

ROLLS-ROYCE PHANTOM DROPHEAD COUPÉ

The Phantom Drophead Coupé is a less formal interpretation of the classic Rolls-Royce design. Its chassis totally constructed in aluminum is both sturdy and light and it combines modern technology with the elegance of a convertible. The timeless Rolls-Royce style dominates its exterior design: a prolonged hood, wheels with a large diameter, and the typical refined and dynamic line that drops over the flanks. The interior design emphasizes the liberty of space. A huge effort was made to achieve pleasant aesthetics and a practical design. High quality materials were used for its construction: wood, leather, chromium and burnished steel. And bleaching agents, dyes and lacquers have been avoided as far as possible in favor of more natural finishes. Despite the apparent simplicity of the design, the car was constructed with a view to high quality driving. The Phantom Drophead Coupé is manufactured with craftsmanship and the best materials and is an example of incomparable technology, design and quality.

El Phantom Drophead Coupé es una interpretación menos formal del diseño Rolls-Royce clásico. A la robustez y ligereza de un bastidor totalmente construido con aluminio, se le suma la tecnología moderna y la elegancia de una carrocería descapotable. En las líneas del exterior destaca el estilo atemporal de los grandes Rolls-Royce: un prolongado capó, ruedas de gran diámetro y la típica, refinada y dinámica línea que desciende por los flancos. En el interior, el diseño destaca la libertad de espacio. Se ha puesto todo el empeño en conseguir una estética agradable y a la vez un diseño práctico. Para su construcción se han empleado materiales de gran calidad: madera, piel, cromo y acero bruñido. Y en la medida de lo posible se han evitado decolorantes, tintes y lacas en favor de acabados más naturales. Tras la sencillez aparente del diseño se encuentra un coche construido para ofrecer una conducción de gran calidad. El Phantom Drophead Coupé presenta una tecnología y un diseño incomparables y está fabricado artesanalmente a partir de los mejores materiales para alcanzar un nivel de calidad sin parangón.

La Phantom Drophead Coupé est une version moins formelle du design classique caractéristique d'une Rolls-Royce. Avec son châssis en aluminium robuste et léger, la technologie moderne se mêle à l'élégance d'une carrosserie décapotable. Ses lignes extérieures particulières reflètent le style intemporel des grandes Rolls-Royce : un capot prolongé, des roues de grand diamètre et cette ligne raffinée et dynamique, caractéristique de la marque. Le de-sign intérieur met en valeur son habitabilité. Tout a été mis en œuvre pour obtenir à la fois une esthétique agréable et un design fonctionnel. Pour sa construction, des matériaux de grande qualité ont été utilisés : bois, cuir, chrome et acier brossé. Dans la mesure du possible, les produits décolorants, les teintures et les laques ont été évités au profit de finitions plus naturelles. Malgré la simplicité apparente du design, la voiture a été conçue pour offrir une conduite de grande qualité. La Phantom Drophead Coupé présente une technologie et un design incomparables. Elle est fabriquée de manière artisanale avec les meilleurs matériaux afin d'obtenir un niveau de qualité sans commune mesure.

TECHNICAL SPECIFICATIONS

Manufacturer	Rolls-Royce
Price	On request
Contact	www.rolls-roycemotorcars.com
Engine/cylinders/valves per cylinder	V / 12 / 48
Displacement	6,749 cc
Power output	453 bhp/460 ps (DIN)/338 kW at 5,350 rpm
Top speed	149.13 mph | 240 km/h
Acceleration 0-100 km/h	5.7 secs
Dimensions (length, width, height)	18.37 ft | 5.60 m, 6.50 ft | 1.98 m, 5.18 ft | 1.58 m
Wheelbase	10.89 ft | 3.32 m
Unloaded weight	6,724.10 lbs | 3,050 kg
Transmission	ZF 6HP32
Fuel management	Direct injection
Fuel consumption city	N.I.

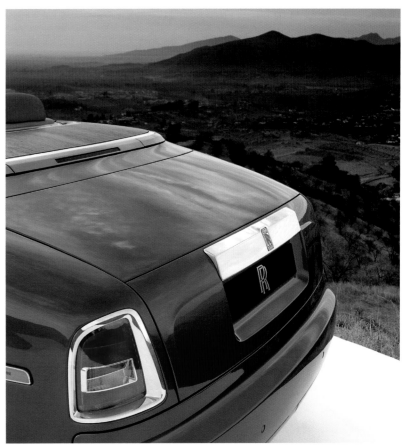

BENTLEY CONTINENTAL GTC

Officially presented in the New York International Auto Show 2006, the Continental GTC is a four-seater convertible with four-wheel drive and a 12 cylinder motor that reaches 194 miles/hour. It is easily handled when driving, has exceptional power, and combines the advantages of a sports car with those of a grand touring car. The interiors are handcrafted and elegant, as is to be expected from this British company, and combine the usual classical touch of leather hides and wood veneers with advanced-technology control panels and functions on the dash. The convertible top, with three layers of fabric and a thermal glass rear window, acts as a highly effective acoustic and thermal insulation and is available in a wide range of colors, both inside and outside. The exclusive four-wheel drive system contributes to the GTC's incredible stability and road grip, while the gear box works both manually and automatically.

Presentado oficialmente en el Salón Internacional del Automóvil de Nueva York de 2006, el Continental GTC es un descapotable de cuatro plazas, con tracción a las cuatro ruedas y un motor de 12 cilindros que permite alcanzar los 312 km/h. De fácil conducción y con una potencia excepcional, el modelo reúne las ventajas de un deportivo y las de un gran turismo. Los interiores, artesanales y elegantes como todos los que acostumbra a ofrecer la firma británica, combinan el habitual toque clásico de la tapicería de cuero y los revestimientos de madera con la avanzada tecnología de paneles y funciones en el salpicadero. La capota, con tres capas de tela y ventana trasera de cristal térmico, es un aislante acústico y térmico maravilloso, y está disponible en una amplia gama de colores, tanto en el interior como en el exterior. El exclusivo sistema de tracción a las cuatro ruedas hace posible una estabilidad y una sujeción a la carretera increíbles, mientras que la caja de cambios funciona tanto manual como automáticamente.

Présentée officiellement au Salon International de l'automobile de New York en 2006, la Continental GTC est une décapotable quatre places, équipée d'une traction à quatre roues motrices et d'un moteur 12 cylindres, qui peut atteindre 312 km/h. A la fois puissante et très facile à conduire, cette voiture réunit les avantages d'un modèle sportif et grand tourisme. Les intérieurs faits main et élégants, caractéristique propre à la marque britannique, associent l'habituelle touche classique des habillages en cuir et des revêtements en bois à la technologie avancée des fonctions du tableau de bord. La capote triple épaisseur en toile et la fenêtre arrière en verre athermique constituent un merveilleux isolant acoustique et thermique. Par ailleurs, plusieurs coloris pour l'extérieur et l'intérieur sont disponibles. Le système de traction à quatre roues motrices exclusif offre une grande stabilité à la GTC et une incroyable tenue de route, avec une boîte de vitesse pouvant fonctionner automatiquement ou manuellement.

TECHNICAL SPECIFICATIONS

Manufacturer	Bentley Motors Limited
Price	€ 219,820
Contact	www.bentleymotors.com
Engine/cylinders/valves per cylinder	6 l W12 Biturbo / N.I. / 4
Displacement	5,998 cc
Power output	552 bhp / 411 kW at 6,100 rpm
Top speed	197.60 mph | 312 km/h
Acceleration 0-100 km/h	4.8 secs
Dimensions (length, width, height)	15.75 ft | 4.80 m, 6.27 ft | 1.91 m, 4.56 ft | 1.39 m
Wheelbase	9.01 ft | 2.75 m
Unloaded weight	5,258 lbs | 2,385 kg
Transmission	6-speed automatic
Fuel management	N.I.
Fuel consumption city	6.92 gal/62.14 mi | 26.2 l/100 km

MERCEDES-BENZ S 65 AMG

The new Mercedes-Benz S 65 AMG is a powerful vehicle whose dual-turbo motor AMG 6 1 V12 is an envied feature of many sports cars. It accelerates from 0 to 62.14 mi/h in 4.4 seconds and from 0 to 124.28 mi/h in just 13.3 seconds (approximate figures). All its other features also respond to high quality standards. The brakes, for example, have a new design, based on the Adaptive Brake system that marks new standards in durability, sensitivity and braking distance. The suspension, with Active Body Control, is the perfect complement for this car's sophisticated driving technology as it reduces movement upon starting, taking corners and braking. Its sporty outer design continues on the inside. The Exclusive Passion leather upholstery and the exclusive ergonomic designer seats create a distinguished style in this extraordinary machine with a powerful driving system.

El nuevo Mercedes-Benz S 65 AMG es un potente vehículo cuyo motor AMG 6 l V12 biturbo es el sueño de muchos coches deportivos. Acelera de 0 a 100 km/h en 4,4 segundos y de 0 a 200 km/h en sólo 13,3 segundos (cifras provisionales). Otras características del vehículo también responden a unos patrones de alta calidad. Los frenos, por ejemplo, tienen un nuevo diseño basado en el sistema Adaptive Brake que marca nuevos estándares de durabilidad, sensibilidad y distancia de frenado. La suspensión, con el sistema Active Body Control, es el complemento perfecto para una tecnología de conducción tan sofisticada como la de este coche y reduce la mayoría de los movimientos derivados de la conducción, como los que se producen al arrancar, al tomar las curvas y al frenar. La línea deportiva del diseño exterior también se encuentra en el interior. La tapicería de piel Exclusive Passion y los asientos de diseño exclusivo y ergonómico aportan un estilo distinguido a esta extraordinaria máquina con un sistema de conducción poderoso.

La nouvelle Mercedes-Benz S 65 AMG est un puissant véhicule doté d'un moteur AMG 6 l V12 bi-turbo que beaucoup de voitures de sport rêveraient d'avoir sous leur capot. Elle passe de 0 à 100 km/h en 4,4 secondes et de 0 à 200 km/h en seulement 13,3 secondes (chiffres provisoires). Les autres caractéristiques du véhicule correspondent également à des critères haut de gamme. Les freins, par exemple, se distinguent par leur nouveau design basé sur le système Adaptive Brake, qui répond aux nouveaux standards de durabilité, de sensibilité et de distance de freinage. La suspension, dotée du système Active Body Control, complète parfaitement la technologie de conduite de cette voiture si sophistiquée. En effet, cette technologie réduit la plupart des mouvements liés à la conduite, comme ceux engendrés par le démarrage, les virages ou le freinage. La ligne sport qui caractérise le design extérieur est également présente dans le design intérieur. La sellerie en cuir Exclusive Passion, ainsi que le design exclusif et ergonomique des sièges, donnent un style élégant à cette extraordinaire berline, dotée d'un puissant système de conduite.

TECHNICAL SPECIFICATIONS

Manufacturer	Mercedes-Benz
Price	From € 236,500
Contact	www.mercedes-benz.com
Engine/cylinders/valves per cylinder	V12 / 12 / 3
Displacement	5,980 cc
Power output	450 kW/612 hp
Top speed	155.34 mph	250 km/h
Acceleration 0-100 km/h	4.4 secs
Dimensions (length, width, height)	17.06 ft	5.20 m, 6.14 ft	1.87 m, 4.82 ft	1.47 m
Wheelbase	10.37 ft	3.16 m
Average weight	4,960 lbs	2,250 kg
Transmission	Manual/automatic
Fuel capacity	23.77 gal	90 l
Fuel consumption city	3.94 gal/62.14 mi	14.9 l/100 km

MASERATI QUATTROPORTE

The Maserati Quattroporte is a vehicle equipped with the most advanced technology. Winner of 25 international prizes, its prestige and luxurious design make taking the wheel a unique experience in inspirational driving. It is available in two versions which offer two different types of driving; the Quattroporte Automatic is apt for a more relaxed driving style and the Quattroporte DuoSelect is more sporty. The motor, the transmission and the active and passive safety devices make this model an excellent and reliable machine. The car has an exceptionally designed interior and a level of comfortable that is on a par with the incomparable pleasure experienced when driven. The materials and finishes are all of the highest quality. Some examples are Tanganyika wood and the Poltrona Frau leather upholstery. The seats are adjusted electronically and have 14 different positions and three memories. Many of the car's characteristics, such as the upholstery or the color can be personalized; moreover the seats have a massage option. Other options such as television and DVD can also be included.

El Maserati Quattroporte es un vehículo equipado con la más avanzada tecnología. Ganador de 25 premios internacionales, su prestigio y su lujoso diseño hacen que llevar su timón sea una experiencia única. Está disponible en dos versiones, el Quattroporte Automatic y el Quattroporte DuoSelect, que proporcionan dos tipos de conducción diferentes, una más relajada y otra más deportiva. El motor, la transmisión y las medidas de seguridad, tanto activas como pasivas, hacen de este modelo una máquina excelente y fiable. Pero no sólo proporciona un placer inigualable al conducirlo, también posee un interior excepcional, confortable y con un fantástico diseño. Los materiales y acabados son de gran calidad, como la madera de Tanganika y la tapicería de cuero Poltrona Frau. Los asientos se ajustan electrónicamente, con posibilidad de hasta 14 posiciones diferentes y tres memorias. Muchas de las características del coche, como la tapicería y el color, pueden personalizarse; además, los asientos brindan la posibilidad de disfrutar de un agradable masaje a los ocupantes del vehículo. También pueden incluirse otras prestaciones como una televisión y un DVD.

La Maserati Quattroporte est un véhicule doté de la technologie la plus moderne. Vainqueur de 25 prix internationaux, son prestige, sa conduite inspiratrice et son luxueux design rendent unique l'expérience passée au volant de cette voiture. Deux versions sont disponibles : la Quattroporte Automatic et la Quattroporte DuoSelect. Elles proposent deux types de conduite distincts : une plus reposante et une autre plus sportive. Le moteur, la transmission et l'équipement de sécurité, actif et passif, font de ce modèle une voiture excellente et fiable. Elle ne procure pas seulement un plaisir inégalable au niveau de la conduite, mais possède également un habitacle exceptionnel, confortable et un design fantastique. Les matériaux et les finitions utilisés, comme le bois de Tanganika ou les garnitures de siège en cuir Poltrona Frau, sont de grande qualité. Les sièges peuvent se régler électroniquement et offrent 14 positions différentes dont trois peuvent être mémorisées. Un grand nombre des caractéristiques de cette voiture, comme les garnitures des sièges ou la couleur, peuvent être personnalisées. Par ailleurs, les sièges peuvent offrir un agréable massage aux occupants du véhicule. D'autres options, comme l'installation d'un téléviseur ou d'un lecteur DVD, peuvent également être choisies.

TECHNICAL SPECIFICATIONS

Manufacturer	Maserati
Price	€ 123,527
Contact	www.maserati.com
Engine/cylinders/valves per cylinder	V8 / 8 / 4
Displacement	4,244 cc
Power output	295 kW
Top speed	166.53 mph | 268 km/h
Acceleration 0-100 km/h	5.6 secs
Dimensions (length, width, height)	16.57 ft | 5.05 m, 6.22 ft | 1.89 m, 4.72 ft | 1.43 m
Wheelbase	10.05 ft | 3.06 m
Unloaded weight	4,100.60 lbs | 1,860 kg
Transmission	Two versions: Automatic and DuoSelect
Fuel capacity	23.77 gal | 90 l
Fuel consumption city	3.88 gal/62.14 mi | 14.7 l/100 km

BMW M6 CABRIO

The BMW M6 convertible model is one of the most impressive sports cars on the market. While guaranteeing comfort that is typical of a great four-seater sports car, its aerodynamic design and its V10 motor (capable of more than 8,000 revolutions) mean that it gives a literally incomparable performance. The convertible top of this cabrio has been designed with an exclusive acoustic insulation system with side parts conceived especially so as not to increase the air penetration coefficient. Innumerable circuit tests were carried out to optimize the BMW M6, which offers an incredibly stable drive (without detriment to power), made easy to a large degree by the Sequential M Transmission SMG with Drivelogic. Moreover, it offers the driver comforts such as the Head-up-Display virtual display system that monitors all the necessary information from the dash. Given its great power, the M6 brake system has the same features as racing cars, with perforated discs that allow it to come to a halt at 62 miles/h in a distance of 118 ft.

La variante descapotable del BMW M6 es uno de los deportivos más impactantes del mercado. Aun garantizando las condiciones de confort propias de un gran deportivo de cuatro plazas, su línea aerodinámica y su motor V10, capaz de revolucionar más allá de las 8.000 vueltas, lo llevan a ofrecer un rendimiento literalmente incomparable. La capota ha sido diseñada con un exclusivo sistema de aislamiento acústico y cuenta con prolongaciones laterales concebidas especialmente para no aumentar su coeficiente de penetración del aire. El BMW M6, cuyas prestaciones han sido optimizadas gracias a innumerables pruebas en circuito, ofrece una conducción increíblemente estable, sin detrimento de la potencia, facilitada en gran parte por el cambio de marchas secuencial SMG mediante el sistema Drivelogic. Además, brinda al conductor comodidades como el sistema de pantalla virtual Head-up-Display, que monitoriza toda la información necesaria desde el salpicadero. Dada su gran potencia, el sistema de frenos del M6 cuenta con las mismas prestaciones que los coches de carreras; entre ellas, los discos perforados compuestos que le permiten disponer de una distancia de frenado de 36 m a 100 km/h.

La variante décapotable de la BMW M6 est l'un des modèles les plus spectaculaires du marché. Bien qu'il garantisse les conditions de confort propres à un modèle sportif quatre places, sa ligne aérodynamique et son moteur V10, capable de dépasser les 8 000 tours minute, permettent d'offrir un rendement tout simplement inégalable. La capote de cette version cabriolet est équipée du meilleur système d'isolation acoustique et dotée de prolongations latérales, spécialement conçues pour augmenter le coefficient de pénétration dans l'air. Améliorée grâce à de nombreux essais réalisés sur circuit, la BMW M6 offre une conduite incroyablement stable sans négliger la puissance, facilitée en grande partie par la boîte de vitesses séquentielle SMG, associée au système Drivelogic. Par ailleurs, le conducteur bénéficie de tout le confort nécessaire, tel que le système d'écran virtuel Head-up-Display qui gère toutes les informations utiles depuis le tableau de bord. Etant donné sa grande puissance, le système de freins de la M6 est équipé de disques perforés comme pour les voitures de course ; la distance de freinage de ce véhicule lancé à 100 km/h est de 36 m.

TECHNICAL SPECIFICATIONS

Manufacturer	BMW
Price	€ 129,500
Contact	www.bmw.com
Engine/cylinders/valves per cylinder	373 kW-507 CV / 10 / 4
Displacement	4,999 cc
Power output	74.6 kW/1,000 cc
Top speed	155.34 mph | 250 km/h
Acceleration 0-100 km/h	4.8 secs
Dimensions (length, width, height)	15.98 ft | 4.87 m, 6 ft | 1.85 m, 4.5 ft | 1.37 m
Wheelbase	255/40 ZR19 front; 285/35 ZR19 rear
Average weight	4,420 lbs | 2,005 kg
Transmission	M7, BMW SMG III 247
Fuel management	N.I.
Fuel consumption city	6 gal/62.14 mi | 22.8 l/100 km

MAYBACH 62

The success of the 62 model has meant that the Maybach company has regained its prestigious position as one of the most elegant and discerning automobile companies in the world, 60 years after its golden age. The Maybach 62 is a deluxe limousine with a length of more than 20 ft, an exceptionally low consumption considering its weight and size, and an engine that allows it, amongst other skills to accelerate from 0 to 62 miles/hour in just under 5 seconds. The individual seats recline into a horizontal position at the press of a button, and provide occupants with maximum relaxation while they are entertained by a DVD system with an integrated audiovisual system, or while they contemplate the sky through the transparent panoramic roof. The Maybach 62 series has infinite details that include special containers for glasses, cups and champagne bottles and even a fitted fridge. Lovers of luxury and exclusivity will no doubt be impressed by the array of glove compartments, desks and various communication systems that transform the Maybach 62 into a fully equipped mobile office.

Gracias al éxito de su modelo 62, la firma Maybach recuperó su prestigio como una de las compañías automovilísticas más elegantes y exigentes del mundo, 60 años después de su época de mayor gloria. El Maybach 62 es una limusina gran clase de más de 6 m de largo, con un consumo excepcionalmente bajo para su peso y tamaño, y un motor que le permite, entre otras proezas, pasar de 0 a 100 km/h en poco más de 5 segundos. Los asientos individuales se reclinan hasta alcanzar la posición horizontal con sólo presionar un botón, y permiten una máxima relajación a sus ocupantes mientras ven un DVD gracias al sistema audiovisual integrado, o mientras contemplan el cielo a través del techo panorámico transparente. Entre los incontables detalles de serie que ofrece el Maybach 62, cabe mencionar los contenedores especiales para vasos, copas y botellas de champán y el frigorífico empotrado. Quienes busquen el mayor grado de lujo y exclusividad se verán sin duda recompensados con la extensa variedad de guanteras, mesas de trabajo y diversos sistemas de comunicación que transforman el Maybach 62 en una oficina móvil muy completa.

Grâce au succès de son modèle 62, l'entreprise Maybach a retrouvé son prestige de constructeur automobile des plus élégants et exigeants au monde, 60 ans après sa période de gloire. La Maybach 62 est une berline de grande classe, de plus de 6 m de long. Elle se distingue par sa consommation exceptionnellement faible pour son poids et sa taille, et son moteur lui permet notamment de passer de 0 à 100 km/h en un peu plus de 5 secondes. En pressant un simple bouton, les sièges individuels peuvent s'incliner en position horizontale offrant ainsi à ses occupants une relaxation optimale lorsqu'ils regardent un DVD, diffusé grâce au système audiovisuel intégré, ou lorsqu'ils contemplent le ciel à travers le toit panoramique transparent. Parmi la multitude d'équipements de série offerts par la Maybach 62, il convient de mentionner les compartiments réservés aux verres, coupes et bouteilles de champagne, ainsi que le réfrigérateur encastré. Les personnes qui recherchent le plus grand luxe possible et l'exclusivité se verront sans aucun doute comblées par ce véhicule doté d'un grand nombre de boîtes à gants, de plusieurs tables de travail et de divers systèmes de communication, qui font de la Maybach 62 un bureau mobile complètement équipé.

TECHNICAL SPECIFICATIONS

Manufacturer	Maybach
Price	€ 360,000
Contact	www.maybach-manufaktur.com
Engine/cylinders/valves per cylinder	V / 12 / 3
Displacement	5,513 cc
Power output	550 bhp
Top speed	155.34 mph | 250 km/h
Acceleration 0-100 km/h	5.4 secs
Dimensions (length, width, height)	20.21 ft | 6.16 m, 6.50 ft | 1.98 m, 5.15 ft | 1.57 m
Wheelbase	12.53 ft | 3.82 m
Unloaded weight	6,294.20 lbs | 2,855 kg
Transmission	T5-speed, automatic
Fuel feed	Electronic fuel injection
Fuel consumption city	4.20 gal/62.14 mi | 15.9 l/100 km

JAGUAR XKR

The new Jaguar XKR is an extraordinary vehicle that provides a unique driving experience. The Jaguar Cars' engineers have designed an elegant and magnificent automobile that responds in any situation and at any speed. For example, its manufacture in aluminum has resulted in a lighter, more agile, fun vehicle that is easy to handle. The automatic transmission of six velocities is leader in its category and the gear change takes milliseconds thanks to the sophisticated levy system. Occupants will find that the interior design, besides its impeccable aesthetics, has ergonomic features and a useful, simple and very intuitive technology. The exclusive sports design seats allow 16 different positions. The Jaguar XKR incorporates a series of aesthetic details that emphasize its sporting nature. For example, the interior Luxury Sport version offers leather seats, and leather finishes on the instrument panel, the doors and the central dashboard.

El nuevo Jaguar XKR es un vehículo extraordinario que proporciona una experiencia de conducción única. Los ingenieros de Jaguar Cars han diseñado un automóvil elegante y soberbio que responde en cualquier situación y a cualquier velocidad. Por ejemplo, la fabricación íntegra en aluminio ha dado como resultado un vehículo más ligero, ágil, divertido y fácil de conducir. La transmisión automática de seis velocidades es líder en su categoría y el cambio de marchas es cuestión de milisegundos gracias a las levas. El diseño del interior, además de tener una estética impecable, presenta unas características ergonómicas y una tecnología útil, sencilla y muy intuitiva, todo al servicio de los ocupantes. Los exclusivos asientos, que permiten 16 posiciones, son de diseño deportivo. El Jaguar XKR incorpora una serie de detalles estéticos que realzan su aspecto deportivo. Por ejemplo, en su versión de interior Luxury Sport, los asientos son de piel, así como los acabados del panel de instrumentos, de las puertas y de la consola central.

Le nouveau modèle Jaguar XKR est un véhicule extraordinaire qui fait de la conduite une expérience unique. Les ingénieurs de Jaguar Cars ont conçu une automobile élégante et somptueuse, répondant à toutes les situations de route quelle que soit la vitesse. Par exemple sa caisse tout en aluminium a permis d'obtenir un véhicule très léger, souple, amusant et facile à conduire. La transmission automatique à six vitesses est la première de sa catégorie et le changement des vitesses est une question d'un millième de seconde grâce aux cames. En plus de se son esthétique impeccable, le design intérieur de cette voiture présente des caractéristiques ergonomiques et une technologie fonctionnelle, simple et très intuitive. Tous ces éléments sont mis au service du conducteur et des passagers. Les sièges exclusifs offrent 16 positions différentes et se distinguent par leur design sportif. La Jaguar XKR offre une série de détails esthétiques qui lui confèrent cette allure sportive. Ainsi l'intérieur de la Luxury Sport est doté de sièges en cuir et des finitions, également en cuir, habillent le tableau de bord, les portes et la console centrale.

TECHNICAL SPECIFICATIONS

Manufacturer	Jaguar
Price	€ 114,400
Contact	www.jaguar.com
Engine/cylinders/valves per cylinder	4.2 V8 / 8 / 4
Displacement	4,196 cc
Power output	240 CV
Top speed	155.34 mph | 250 km/h
Acceleration 0-100 km/h	5.2 secs
Dimensions (length, width, height)	15.72 ft | 4.79 m, 6.20 ft | 1.89 m, 4.33 ft | 1.32 m
Wheelbase	9.02 ft | 2.75 m
Unloaded weight	3,670.7 lbs | 1,665 kg
Transmission	Automatic
Fuel capacity	18.78 gal | 71.1 l
Fuel consumption city	3.25 gal /62.14 mi| 12.3 l/100 km

159

PORSCHE CARRERA GT

The Carrera GT takes power and the sporting spirit to new dimensions. It is the first vehicle in the world to be equipped with a ceramic clutch. It is a tremendously competitive machine that stands out for its almost impossible features and advanced technology. It does not need ESP, launch control launch, overfeed, adjustable bodywork and four-wheel drive, the model focuses on essential race winning elements. The use of light materials such as the carbon fiber reinforced plastic bodywork keep the weight of the Carrera GT below 3,042 lbs. Thus it can accelerate to 62 miles/hour in 3.9 seconds and has a top speed of 205 miles/hour. Even so, the Carrera GT transmits the stability and equilibrium that is expected of a Porsche. Its 10 cylinder mechanics are also notable with dry sump lubrication, based on the well-known V10 normal-aspiration engine, with the characteristic of an increased cylinder capacity from 1.45 to 1.5 gallons. This engine can develop a maximum power of 612 CV at 8,000 rpm with a par value of 590 Nm.

La potencia y el espíritu deportivo llegan a su máxima expresión con el Carrera GT, el primer vehículo del mundo equipado con un embrague cerámico. Se trata de una máquina tremendamente competitiva que destaca por unas prestaciones de ensueño y una avanzada tecnología. Prescindiendo de ESP, *control launch*, sobrealimentación, chasis regulable y tracción a las cuatro ruedas, el modelo se concentra en lo esencial para cumplir con la misión de ganar carreras. Gracias al empleo de materiales ligeros, como la carrocería de plástico reforzado con fibra de carbono, el Carrera GT no sobrepasa los 1.380 kg. Así es como logra ponerse a 100 km/h en 3,9 segundos y alcanza una velocidad punta de 330 km/h. A pesar de ello, el Carrera GT transmite la estabilidad y el equilibrio que se espera de un modelo de Porsche. También destaca su mecánica de 10 cilindros con lubricación por cárter seco, basada en el conocido motor V10 de aspiración normal, con la particularidad de una cilindrada incrementada de 5,5 a 5,7 litros. Este motor desarrolla una potencia máxima de 612 CV a 8.000 rpm, con un par de 590 Nm.

Avec la Carrera GT, Porsche a atteint la perfection en ce qui concerne la puissance et l'esprit sportif d'un véhicule, le premier au monde à être équipée d'un embrayage en céramique. Il s'agit d'une machine extrêmement compétitive, qui se distingue par ses prestations de rêve et sa technologie avancée : Dépourvu d'ESP, *control launch*, suralimentation, châssis réglable ou traction quatre roues motrices, le modèle se concentre sur l'essentiel : décrocher la victoire dans une course automobile. Grâce à l'utilisation de matériaux légers, comme la carrosserie en plastique renforcée par des fibres de carbone, la Carrera GT ne dépasse pas les 1 380 kg. Elle peut passer de 0 à 100 km/h en 3,9 secondes et sa vitesse de pointe atteint 330 km/h. Ce qui ne l'empêche pas d'offrir toute la stabilité et l'équilibre que l'on peut attendre d'un modèle conçu par Porsche. Ce véhicule se distingue également par sa mécanique dotée de dix cylindres à lubrification à carter sec déclinée du célèbre moteur V10 de 5,5 litres. Porté à 5,7 litres, son moteur développe une puissance maximale de 612 CV à 8 000 tr/min, avec un couple de 590 Nm.

TECHNICAL SPECIFICATIONS

Manufacturer	Porsche
Price	€ 452,690
Contact	www.porsche.com
Engine/cylinders/valves per cylinder	V / 10 / 4
Displacement	5,733 cc
Power output	612 CV
Top speed	205.05 mph | 330 km/h
Acceleration 0-100 km/h	3.9 secs
Dimensions (length, width, height)	15.12 ft | 4.61 m, 6.30 ft | 1.92 m, 3.81 ft | 1.16 m
Wheelbase	8.96 ft | 2.73 m
Unloaded weight	3,042 lbs | 1,380 kg
Transmission	6-speed, manual
Fuel feed	Port injection
Fuel consumption city	4.70 gal/62.14 mi | 17.8 l/100 km

FERRARI FERRARI ENZO

Ferrari's new sporty two-seater was conceived in honor of Enzo Anselmo Ferrari, the founder of the prancing horse motor-racing team. Designed in its totality by the legendary Pininfarina, it takes over from the F50. With a limited production run of 349 cars, the new Enzo is equipped with carbon fiber bodywork, a suspension system very similar to that used in Formula 1 and gull-wing doors that pivot forwards at just the push of a button. It has a power of 660 CV, accelerates from 0 to 62 miles/h in 3.65 seconds and reaches a maximum speed of 217 miles/hour. Safety and grip are guaranteed thanks to the innovative suspension with variable height and the carbon disc brakes developed by Brembo. Lacking a gear stick, this two-seater renounces unnecessary luxuries in its interior. The large sporty steering wheel, also inspired by the Formula 1 range, and the anatomic carbon fiber and red leather chairs are also worth a mention.

Bautizado en homenaje a Enzo Anselmo Ferrari, fundador de la escudería del caballo rampante, y diseñado íntegramente por el legendario Pininfarina, el nuevo deportivo biplaza de Ferrari toma el relevo del F50. Con una producción limitada de 349 coches, el nuevo Enzo está equipado con carrocería de fibra de carbono, un sistema de suspensión muy parecido al empleado en la Fórmula 1 y puertas plegables que pivotan hacia delante con sólo pulsar un botón. Con una potencia de 660 CV, va de 0 a 100 km/h en 3,65 segundos y alcanza los 350 km/h de velocidad máxima. La seguridad y la adherencia al suelo están garantizadas gracias a la innovadora suspensión de altura variable y a los frenos de discos de carbono desarrollados por Brembo. Desprovisto de palanca de cambios, este biplaza renuncia en su interior a los lujos innecesarios. Cabe destacar el volante deportivo de gran tamaño, inspirado también en la Fórmula 1, y los asientos anatómicos de fibra de carbono y cuero rojo.

Baptisé ainsi en hommage à Enzo Anselmo Ferrari, fondateur de l'écurie au cheval cabré, le nouveau modèle sportif biplace a été entièrement dessiné par le légendaire Pininfarina. Avec une production limitée à 349 exemplaires, la nouvelle Enzo est équipée d'une carrosserie en fibre de carbone, d'un système de suspension semblable à ceux utilisés en Formule 1 et de portes pliantes qui pivotent vers l'avant en appuyant sur un simple bouton. Avec une puissance de 660 CV, elle peut passer de 0 à 100 km/h en 3,65 secondes et sa vitesse maximale peut atteindre les 350 km/h. La sécurité et la tenue de route sont garanties par une suspension novatrice à hauteur variable et des disques de freins en carbone, développés pour Brembo. L'habitacle de ce biplace dépourvu de levier de vitesse renonce à tout luxe superflu. Il est important de mentionner le volant de grande taille, inspiré des Formules 1, et les sièges anatomiques en fibre de carbone et en cuir rouge.

TECHNICAL SPECIFICATIONS

Manufacturer	Ferrari
Price	€ 645,000
Contact	www.ferrariworld.com
Engine/cylinders/valves per cylinder	V / 12 / 4
Displacement	5,998 cc
Power output	660 CV
Top speed	217.4 mph	350 km/h
Acceleration 0-100 km/h	3.65 secs
Dimensions (length, width, height)	15.42 ft	4.70 m, 6.66 ft	2.03 m, 3.74 ft	1.14 m
Wheelbase	8.69 ft	2.65 m
Unloaded weight	3,009.31 lbs	1,365 kg
Transmission	6-speed, manual
Fuel feed	Bosch Motronic ME7 fuel injection
Fuel consumption city	8.08 gal/62.14 mi	30.6 l/100 km

CORVETTE Z06

The outer design of the Corvette Z06 is a combination of the company's classical lines with the appeal of a newly designed sports car. The Z06 coupé and convertible versions have an unmistakable design, characterized by the wide front and the large forward-facing grille. The bodywork aerodynamics is a result of Corvette's racing experiences, where stability at high speed and behavior in corners are key factors. Another distinctive feature is the smaller steering wheel, which also exists in other Corvettes, and is aimed at making turning easier and giving a sportier drive. Although it is designed with the features of a precision vehicle, the Z06 also performs highly in day to day driving. Comfort and convenience were priority objectives: HID headlamps, anti-fog lights, leather seats, dual zone air conditioning, integrated upper projection screen are just some of the series components that are included.

El diseño exterior del Corvette Z06 combina las líneas clásicas y la nueva expresividad del diseño deportivo propias de la marca. El Z06 tiene un diseño inconfundible, tanto en su versión *coupé* como en la descapotable, en la que destaca su amplio frontal con una gran abertura en la parrilla orientada hacia delante. La aerodinámica de la carrocería proviene de las experiencias del programa de competición de Corvette, donde la estabilidad con altas velocidades y el comportamiento en las curvas son factores clave. Otro rasgo distintivo es el volante más pequeño, que también presentan otros Corvette, pensado para una mayor maniobrabilidad y una conducción deportiva. Aunque está diseñado con las características de un vehículo de precisión, el Z06 también ofrece un alto rendimiento en la conducción cotidiana. Para este fin, el confort era un objetivo prioritario: faros HID, luces antiniebla, asientos de cuero, aire acondicionado bizona y pantalla de proyección superior integrada son algunos de los componentes que vienen incorporados de serie.

Le design extérieur de la Corvette Z06 associe les lignes classiques et la nouvelle expression du design sportif propres à la marque. Les versions coupé et décapotable de la Z06 ont un design incomparable. La décapotable se distingue par l'amplitude de la partie avant, avec une grande ouverture dans le bouclier avant. L'aérodynamique de la carrosserie a été obtenue grâce aux expériences du programme de compétition de Corvette, qui privilégie des facteurs tels que la stabilité à grande vitesse et la tenue de route. Egalement présent sur d'autres modèles de la marque, le volant, plus petit, constitue un trait distinctif supplémentaire. Il a été conçu pour appréhender les virages plus facilement et pour offrir au conducteur une conduite plus sportive. Bien que la Z06 ait été conçue pour répondre aux caractéristiques d'un véhicule de grande précision, elle est également très satisfaisante au quotidien. C'est pourquoi ses objectifs prioritaires résident dans son confort et sa fonctionnalité : phares HID, feux antibrouillard, sièges en cuir, climatisation double zone et écran de projection intégré viennent compléter la liste des équipements de série.

TECHNICAL SPECIFICATIONS

Manufacturer	Corvette
Price	From € 54,000 to € 88,450
Contact	www.chevrolet.com/corvette
Engine/cylinders/valves per cylinder	7.0l V8 / N.I. / 2
Displacement	N.I.
Power output	377 kW
Top speed	198.84 mph	320 km/h
Acceleration 0-100 km/h	3.8 secs
Dimensions (length, width, height)	14.60 ft	4.45 m, 6.30 ft	1.92 m, 4.07 ft	1.24 m
Wheelbase	8.79 ft	2.68 m
Unloaded weight	3,126.16 lbs	1,418 kg
Transmission	Six-speed manual Tremec
Fuel management	18.17 gal	68.8 l
Fuel consumption city	6.02 gal/62.14 mi	22.8 l/100 km

LAMBORGHINI Gallardo Superleggera

The "light" version of the Gallardo model reduces the total weight of the sports car by 220 pounds and increases the power of its motor by 10 hp. It takes just 3.8 seconds to accelerate from 0 to 62 miles/h, and is undeniably the fastest model in its range. The production volume of this model is even more exclusive than that of the normal Gallardo due to its outstanding nature within the manufacturer's already excellent catalog. The carbon fiber bodywork follows the Lamborghini line of elegance and unbeatable aerodynamics. The trunk however combines this material with transparent polycarbonate that provides an even greater lightness. The motor is the last version of the well-known 4,961 cc V10, but it has improved its volumetric efficiency resulting in even greater power. It is available in four colors: yellow, orange, gray and black. The Gallardo Superleggera has various optional features including a rear video camera to ease parking, sports spoiler, safety belts with four grip points and a multimedia system with automatic CD change.

La versión «ligera» del modelo Gallardo reduce en 100 kg el peso total del deportivo y aumenta la potencia de su motor en 10 hp. Con una marca de sólo 3,8 segundos para llegar de 0 a 100 km/h, es, con diferencia, el modelo más rápido de su gama. Por su excelencia dentro del ya excelente catálogo de la marca, el volumen de producción de este modelo es aún más exclusivo que el del Gallardo habitual. La carrocería de fibra de carbono sigue en la línea de la elegancia e insuperable aerodinámica de todos los Lamborghini, pero el capó combina este material con un policarbonato transparente que aporta incluso mayor ligereza al conjunto. El motor es la última versión del conocido 4.961 cc V10 de la marca, pero se ha mejorado su eficacia volumétrica, con lo que se ha conseguido una potencia todavía mayor. Disponible en cuatro colores —amarillo, naranja, gris y negro—, el Gallardo Superleggera ofrece la posibilidad de incorporar, entre otras prestaciones, una videocámara trasera para facilitar el aparcado, un alerón deportivo, unos cinturones de seguridad con cuatro puntos de agarre y un sistema multimedia con cambiador automático de CD.

La version « légère » du modèle Gallardo fait 100 kilos de moins (poids total) et la puissance du moteur a été augmentée de 10 CV. Seules 3,8 secondes sont nécessaires à son moteur pour atteindre les 100 km/h, ce qui fait de ce modèle le plus rapide de sa catégorie. Se distinguant des autres modèles d'excellence de la marque, son rendement est encore plus impressionnant que celui de la Gallardo classique. La carrosserie en fibre de carbone assure la continuité de l'élégance et la supériorité de l'aérodynamique de toutes les Lamborghini. Le capot associe également ce matériau à du polycarbonate transparent, ce qui allège encore l'ensemble. Le moteur correspond à la dernière version du V10 4 961 cc, mais son efficacité volumétrique a été améliorée, afin d'obtenir une puissance supérieure. Disponible en jaune, orange, gris et noir, la Gallardo Superleggera offre des options telles qu'une caméra de recul pour faciliter les créneaux, un aileron sportif, des ceintures de sécurité quatre points ainsi qu'un système multimédia avec changeur CD.

TECHNICAL SPECIFICATIONS

Manufacturer	Lamborghini
Price	€ 157,650
Contact	www.lamborghini.com
Engine/cylinders/valves per cylinder	N.I. / 10 / 4
Displacement	4,961 cc
Power output	520 ps (512 hp, 382 kW) at 8,000 rpm
Top speed	195.11 mph | 314 km/h
Acceleration 0-100 km/h	3.8 secs
Dimensions (length, width, height)	14.11 ft | 4.30 m, 6.23 ft | 1.90 m, 3.87 ft | 1.18 m
Wheelbase	8.4 ft | 2.56 m
Unloaded weight	3,461 lbs | 1,570 kg
Transmission	Permanent all-wheel drive with Viscous Clutch
Fuel management	Multipoint sequential fuel injection
Fuel consumption city	6.55 gal/62.14 mi | 24.8 l/100 km

HUMMER H2 SPECIAL EDITION

Hummers are elegant four-wheel drive vehicles with resistant features. The model presented in these pages is the H2 Special Edition, in a glacial blue color. This vehicle has all the features expected from a car of its category: exceptional power and great precision. The suspension guarantees control and comfort in both road and off-road driving. The power comes from the standard 6-liter Vortec V-8 motor that generates 325 horse power. The tracking control and the anti-block brake system facilitate maximum control on slippery surfaces. Moreover the ABS system can detect and adjust braking on gravel surfaces or on surface areas with potholes. If necessary, the traction control system can use traction in just one wheel. The resistant exterior gives way to a luxurious interior that has heated leather seats with electronic adjustment. Moreover, other features complete this versatile vehicle, such as GPS, DVD in the back seats and rear vision camera system.

Los Hummer son unos coches todoterreno elegantes y de rasgos duros. El modelo que se presenta en estas páginas es el H2 Special Edition, en color azul glacial. Este vehículo ofrece todas las prestaciones que se esperan de un coche de su categoría: una fuerza excepcional y una gran precisión. La suspensión garantiza el control y la comodidad en la circulación tanto por carretera como por campo abierto. La potencia procede del motor estándar Vortec V-8 de 6 litros que genera 325 CV. El control de tracción y los frenos antibloqueo facilitan un control óptimo en las superficies resbaladizas. Además, el sistema ABS puede detectar y ajustar el frenado en terrenos con gravilla o en una superficie con baches. Si es necesario, el sistema de control de tracción consigue tracción en una sola rueda. El resistente exterior da paso a un interior de lujo que dispone de asientos de cuero con calefacción y ajuste electrónico. Además, cuenta con otras prestaciones que completan este versátil vehículo, como el navegador, el DVD en los asientos posteriores y la cámara del sistema de retrovisión.

Les Hummer sont des voitures tout terrain qui se distinguent par une allure agressive et élégante à la fois. Le modèle présenté ici est le H2 bleu glacé Special Edition. Cette voiture offre toutes les prestations que peut présenter un véhicule de cette catégorie : une puissance exceptionnelle et une grande précision. La suspension garantit une maîtrise totale de la conduite ainsi qu'un grand confort, sur route comme sur des terrains accidentés. La puissance de cette voiture est générée par un moteur standard Vortec V-8 de 6 litres et de 325 CV. Le contrôle de traction et le système de freinage antiblocage permettent la maîtrise optimale du véhicule sur les surfaces glissantes. Par ailleurs, le système ABS peut détecter et ajuster le freinage sur des terrains cailouteux ou en cas de nids de poules. Si nécessaire, le système de contrôle de traction s'applique à une seule roue. L'allure robuste du design extérieur dissimule un intérieur luxueux, équipé de sièges en cuir chauffants réglables électroniquement. Par ailleurs, d'autres options complètent ce véhicule polyvalent, comme le GPS, le lecteur-DVD dans les sièges avant ou la caméra de recul.

TECHNICAL SPECIFICATIONS

Manufacturer	Hummer
Price	On request
Contact	www.hummer.com
Engine/cylinders/valves per cylinder	Vorte V-8/N.I./N.I.
Displacement	N.I.
Power output	242 kW at 5200 rpm
Top speed	N.I.
Acceleration 0-100 km/h	N.I.
Dimensions (length, width, height)	17 ft	5.17 m, 6.75 ft	2.06 m, 6.6 ft	2.01 m
Wheelbase	10.2 ft	3.11 m
Unloaded weight	6,413.25 lbs	2,909 kg
Transmission	4-speed Hydra-Matic 4L65
Fuel management	32 gal	121 l
Fuel consumption city	N.I.

HARLEY-DAVIDSON

FLHTCUSE SCREAMIN' EAGLE® ULTRA CLASSIC® ELECTRA RIDE®

The prestigious company Harley-Davidson has developed a program of limited series vehicles, the Custom Vehicle Operations. The motorcycle Screamin' Eagle is a new version within this program. This new motorcycle, of which very few are manufactured, has impressive features, and incomparable style and luxury. The new 1,802 cc Twin Cam 110™ motor dominates the road. The style has been modernized with a new paint design and a new collection of "Ironside" accessories, which include electrically-closed trunks, Tour-Pack knapsacks and a navigation system. The trunks and the knap-packs have an electric block system that is activated by means of a switch on the control panel. The audio navigation system works by GPS and the model includes a series of audio equipment. The driver may enjoy additional comfort thanks to a comfortable and warm seat and leather grips.

La prestigiosa empresa Harley-Davidson ha desarrollado un programa de vehículos de serie limitada, el Custom Vehicle Operations. Dentro de este programa, ofrece una nueva versión de la motocicleta Screamin' Eagle Ultra. Esta nueva moto, de la que se fabrican pocas unidades, tiene unas prestaciones impresionantes, y un estilo y un lujo sin igual. Incorpora el nuevo motor Twin Cam 110™, de 1.802 cc, que consigue dominar la carretera con autoridad. Se ha actualizado su estética con un nuevo diseño de pintura y una nueva colección de accesorios Ironside, entre los que se incluyen maleteros de cerradura eléctrica, alforjas Tour-Pack y un sistema de navegación. Los maleteros y las alforjas incorporan un sistema de bloqueo electrónico que se activa mediante un interruptor situado en el panel de mandos. El sistema de navegación por audio funciona por GPS y el modelo incorpora de serie un equipo de audio. Gracias a un asiento y a unas empuñaduras de cuero cómodas y calientes, el conductor disfruta de mayor confort.

La prestigieuse entreprise Harley-Davidson a développé un programme de véhicules en série limitée, appelé Custom Vehicle Operations, qui propose une nouvelle version de la moto Screamin' Eagle Ultra. Cette nouvelle moto, fabriquée à peu d'exemplaires, offre des performances impressionnantes, un style inégalé et un luxe sans aucune commune mesure. Elle est dotée du nouveau moteur Twin Cam 110™, de 1 802 cc qui lui permet de régner en maître sur les routes. Le style a été modernisé avec une nouvelle peinture et grâce à une nouvelle collection d'accessoires « Ironside », parmi lesquels on trouve des coffres à serrure électrique, des sacoches Tour-Pack et un système de navigation. Les coffres et les sacoches sont équipés d'un système de verrouillage électronique contrôlé grâce à un interrupteur situé sur le tableau de bord. Le système de navigation audio fonctionne par GPS et comprend un équipement audio de série. Une selle et des poignées en cuir chauffantes et fonctionnelles assurent au conducteur un confort supplémentaire.

TECHNICAL SPECIFICATIONS

Manufacturer	Harley-Davidson
Price	€ 38,000
Contact	www.harley-davidson.com
Engine/cylinders/valves per cylinder	1,802 cc/2 V45°/2
Displacement	1,800 cc
Power output	66 kW at 5,000 rpm
Top speed	108.74 mph | 175 km/h
Acceleration 0-100 km/h	N.I.
Dimensions (length, width, height)	8.10 ft | 2.47 m, 3.18 ft | 0.97 m, 4.76 ft | 1.45 m
Wheelbase	5.31 ft | 1.62 m
Unloaded weight	870.83 lbs | 395 kg
Transmission	Cruise Drive 6 gears
Fuel management	5.10 gal | 19.3 l
Fuel consumption city	N.I.

MV Agusta F4 CC

Claudio Castiglioni, managing director of MV, decided to put his initials on the motorcycle he had always dreamed of. He fell into the temptation of creating a really magnificent motorcycle, a unique model. He used all the means available, exclusive materials and the latest technology in order to ensure the vehicle's maximum performance. The motorcycle exterior is elegant and sophisticated thanks to its lines and its black color. This unique motorcycle was lovingly created by Massimo Tamburini from a design that oozes luxury and splendor. However, this machine's exclusivity is what makes it extraordinary; it doesn't matter if it hardly ever leaves the garage, or if it is just used for short distances. What is really exciting is having one of the 100 unique models that should be treated like a priceless work of art. The series numeration has been engraved on a platinum sheet on each machine. Special packaging and a certificate of origin make the delivery of each motorcycle a memorable ceremony.

Claudio Castiglioni, director general de MV, decidió poner sus iniciales a la motocicleta con la que siempre había soñado. Cayó en la tentación de crear una moto verdaderamente especial, magnífica, un modelo único. Lógicamente, utilizó todos los medios disponibles a su alcance, materiales exclusivos y la última tecnología para lograr un rendimiento máximo del vehículo. Exteriormente, la motocicleta es elegante y sofisticada gracias a sus líneas y a la presencia del color negro. Única en su género, esta motocicleta fue esculpida por Massimo Tamburini a partir de un diseño que destila lujo y esplendor. Pero lo importante es la exclusividad de esta máquina; poco importa si nunca sale del garaje, o si se utiliza sólo para dar un pequeño paseo. Lo que realmente entusiasma es poseer uno de los 100 únicos modelos y tratarlo como si fuera una pintura de valor incalculable. La numeración de serie se ha grabado en una placa de platino en cada máquina. Además, un embalaje especial y un certificado de origen hacen de la entrega de cada moto una ceremonia memorable.

Claudio Castiglioni, directeur de MV, a décidé d'inscrire ses initiales sur la moto dont il a toujours rêvé. Il a succombé à la tentation de créer une moto réellement atypique et magnifique. Il a bien évidemment utilisé tous les moyens dont il disposait, les matériaux les plus luxueux et la technologie la plus avancée pour assurer à ce véhicule le meilleur rendement. Extérieurement, grâce à ses lignes et à la présence du noir, cette moto est élégante et sophistiquée. Unique en son genre, elle a été conçue par Massimo Tamburini avec luxe et splendeur. Mais le plus important c'est l'exclusivité de cette machine ; peu importe si elle reste au garage ou si elle est simplement utilisée pour faire une petite promenade de temps en temps. Ce qui procure un réel plaisir c'est le fait de posséder l'un des 100 modèles uniques et de le chérir comme s'il s'agissait d'une œuvre d'art d'une valeur inestimable. Chaque machine possède un numéro de série gravé sur une plaque de platine. Par ailleurs, un emballage spécial et un certificat d'origine rendent la livraison de la moto inoubliable.

TECHNICAL SPECIFICATIONS

Manufacturer	MV Agusta
Price	€ 99,600
Contact	www.mvagusta.it
Engine/cylinders/valves per cylinder	"Weber Marelli" 5SM ignition/ 4/ 4
Displacement	1,078 cc
Power output	147 kW
Top speed	195.73 mph | 315 km/h
Acceleration 0-100 km/h	N.I.
Dimensions (length, width, height)	6.56 ft | 2 m, 2.23 ft | 0.68 m, 2.66 ft | 0.81 m
Wheelbase	4.59 ft | 1.40 m
Unloaded weight	412.26 lbs | 187 kg
Transmission	Cassete gearbox, 6 speed
Fuel capacity	5.55 gal | 21 l
Fuel consumption city	N.I.

DUCATI DESMOSEDICI RR

In the 2006 Mugello Moto Grand Prix, Ducati presented the Ducati Corse Desmosedici GP6 motorcycle. The RR model evolved from this motorcycle, along with the experience gained by Ducati in Moto GP, which enabled them to materialize the dream of uniting technology and performance in a single model beyond reach of their rivals. According to Filippo Preziosi, Managing Director of Ducati Corse, the philosophy of this project is expressed in the total integration of the machine, the chassis and the motorcyclist. This principle shaped the project from the first moment that the challenge was undertaken to design the Ducati Desmosedici. Both the design of the lines and the aerodynamics are true to its predecessor, the Desmosedici GP6. The color, the accessories and the materials used in building it, as well as the technical characteristics of the powerful four-cylinder desmodromic engine, designed by the engineer Borgo Paniale, make a totally convincing motorcycle. The Desmosedici RR is the quintessence of latest generation Moto GP racing machine technology applied to commercial motorcycles. The production line is limited to around 400 units a year and reservations must be made through official Ducati suppliers.

En el Gran Premio de Mugello de 2006 Ducati presentó la motocicleta Ducati Corse Desmosedici GP6. El modelo RR procede de esa motocicleta y materializa el sueño de unir la tecnología y el rendimiento sin competencia, procedentes directamente de la experiencia de Ducati en Moto GP. Según Filippo Preziosi, director general de Ducati Corse, la filosofía de este proyecto se expresa en la integración total de la máquina, el chasis y el motorista. Este concepto básico ha formado parte del proyecto desde el momento en que se abordó el desafío de diseñar la Ducati Desmosedici. Tanto el diseño de las formas como la aerodinámica reflejan fielmente a su antecesora, la Desmosedici GP6. El color, los accesorios y los materiales utilizados en la construcción, así como las características técnicas del potente motor desmodrómico de cuatro cilindros, construido por la ingeniería Borgo Panigale, no dejan lugar a dudas: la Desmosedici RR es la expresión de la última generación de máquinas de Moto GP empleadas en motocicletas comerciales. La producción es limitada, de aproximadamente 400 unidades al año, y debe reservarse a través de distribuidores oficiales Ducati.

Lors du Grand Prix de Mugello 2006, Ducati a présenté la moto Ducati Corse Desmosedici GP6. Le modèle RR provient de cette moto et matérialise le rêve d'unir technologie et performances, issu directement de l'expérience de Ducati en Moto GP. Selon Filippo Preziosi, Directeur Général de Ducati Corse, la philosophie de ce projet s'exprime à travers l'intégration totale de la machine, du châssis et du conducteur. Ce concept de base a régi le projet dès que l'on a relevé le défi de concevoir la Ducati Desmosedici. Aussi bien le design des formes que l'aérodynamique reflètent fidèlement son prédécesseur, la Desmosedici GP6. La couleur, les accessoires, les matériaux utilisés, ainsi que les caractéristiques techniques du puissant moteur *desmodromic* de quatre cylindres construit par l'ingénierie Borgo Paniale ne laissent aucun doute : la Desmosedici RR est l'expression dernier cri des machines de courses Moto GP, appliquée à des motos commerciales. La production est limitée, environ 400 unités par an, et il faut les réserver à travers les distributeurs officiels Ducati.

TECHNICAL SPECIFICATIONS

Manufacturer	Ducati
Price	€ 66,000
Contact	www.ducati.com
Engine/cylinders/valves per cylinder	L-4 cylinder, liquid-cooled, DOHC, desmodromic, gear driven camshafts / 4 / 4
Displacement	989 cc
Power output	More than 200 hp at 13,500 rpm
Top speed	N.I.
Acceleration 0-100 km/h	N.I.
Wheelbase	N.I.
Dimensions (length, width, height)	N.I.
Unloaded weight	N.I.
Transmission	6-speed; cassette type gearbox
Fuel injection	Four 50 mm Magneti Marelli throttle bodies, 12-hole "microjet" with injectors over throttle, manual idle control
Fuel consumption city	N.I.

Luxury flying

Vuelo de lujo

Aviation de luxe

Luxury flying
Vuelo de lujo
Aviation de luxe

Flying in a private jet is a luxury that few can afford. Whether for business or for pleasure, access to this type of transport would suggest a luxurious lifestyle and an elevated status. This form of transport offers multiple advantages. One of the most important is the independence to travel to a destination, however far away, without having to resort to airlines and adapt to their timetables. One can be more spontaneous and impulsive; last-minute decisions to get away are possible if you have a jet. Intimacy and anonymity are also guaranteed when traveling in a private jet. Actors and stars from the world of show business, politicians and high-flying executives frequently use these craft in order to enjoy more peaceful journeys without interruptions. Comfort is another highly valued advantage of flying in these small private jets. No time is lost boarding, checking in suitcases, etc. All seats are business class and the service is always impeccable. The seats, the interior space, the contact with the crew, etc. are all exclusive and personalized. But the real luxury resides in managing and enjoying ones own time. Time is one of the most valuable and consequently most desired goods in modern society, where we are always in a hurry. Traveling in these planes allows one to take advantage of time spent in the air to work, rest or simply chat.

Viajar en avión privado es un lujo al alcance de muy pocos. Ya sea por negocios o por placer, el acceso a este tipo de transporte denota un gran nivel de vida y un elevado estatus. Las ventajas que proporciona este tipo de transporte son múltiples. Una de las más importantes es la independencia para llegar a un destino, por lejano que sea, puesto que deja de ser necesario recurrir a las compañías aéreas y atenerse a sus horarios. Se puede ser más espontáneo e impulsivo; decidir en el último momento hacer una escapada es posible si se dispone de un jet. La intimidad y el anonimato también están garantizados cuando se disfruta de un vuelo en un jet privado. Actores y estrellas del espectáculo, además de políticos y empresarios importantes, utilizan frecuentemente estos aparatos para disfrutar de viajes más tranquilos y sin interrupciones. Otra ventaja muy valorada es la comodidad. No se pierde tiempo con el embarque ni con la facturación de maletas, etc. Todas las plazas son *business class* y el servicio siempre es inmejorable. Los asientos, el espacio del interior, el trato con la tripulación... todo es exclusivo y personalizado. Pero el verdadero lujo reside en el hecho de disfrutar y gestionar el propio tiempo. En la sociedad actual, que nos obliga a las prisas y a la velocidad, el tiempo es uno de los bienes más preciados y, en consecuencia, más deseados. Viajar en estos aviones supone la posibilidad de ganar tiempo y de aprovecharlo durante el vuelo para trabajar, descansar o simplemente conversar.

Voyager en jet privé est un luxe à la portée d'une poignée de personnes. Que se soit pour le travail ou pour le plaisir, l'accès à ce type de transport est synonyme de réussite sociale et d'un niveau économique élevé. Les avantages offerts par ce type de transport sont nombreux. L'indépendance est l'un des plus importants, pour se rendre à une quelconque destination, quelle que soit la distance, il n'est désormais plus nécessaire de faire appel aux compagnies aériennes et de se conformer aux horaires de vol. Cette situation laisse plus de liberté à la spontanéité et aux envies. En effet, si l'on possède un jet, il est possible de décider, au dernier moment, de partir faire une petite escapade. Par ailleurs, lorsque vous profiter d'un vol à bord d'un jet privé, l'intimité et l'anonymat sont garantis. Des acteurs, des stars du monde du spectacle, des hommes politiques et des grands chefs d'entreprise utilisent fréquemment ces appareils pour profiter de voyages plus reposants et sans escales. Voyager à bord de ces petits avions privés apporte un autre avantage hautement apprécié, celui du confort : aucune perte de temps à l'enregistrement, aucun bagage facturé, etc. Toutes les places sont des *business class* et le service est toujours exceptionnel. Les sièges, l'espace intérieur, l'accueil réservé par l'équipage, etc., sont tous exclusifs et personnalisés. Mais le véritable luxe réside dans le fait de pouvoir profiter et de gérer son temps. Dans la société actuelle, où chaque individu doit se presser, le temps est l'une des choses les plus précieuses et par conséquent les plus convoitées. Voyager dans ces avions permet de gagner du temps et de profiter du vol pour travailler, se reposer ou simplement bavarder.

RAYTHEON AIRCRAFT HAWKER 4000

The Hawker 4000 is the pride of Raytheon Aircraft and its creators have correctly claimed it to be the "the most advanced and luxurious super-midsize business jet in the world". Devised to get executives wherever they need to be, whenever they need to be there, the model has a powerful Pratt & Whitney engine that guarantees a range of more than 3,000 nautical miles. In fact, its stability and flight performance are referred to as "best I've ever flown". Honeywell Primus EPIC has created the largest cabin in its class with a large and comfortable private lavatory and an area for luggage and goods that is accessible in flight. Raytheon Aircraft offers a customized interior, according to the client's taste, in terms of number and position of seats, upholstery and wood veneers. The advanced Collins Airshow entertainment electronics make it easy to create a quiet, comfortable environment.

Publicitado, con justicia, por sus creadores como el "*jet* privado de tamaño medio más lujoso del mundo", el Hawker 4000 es el orgullo de Raytheon Aircraft. Pensado para cumplir con creces la misión de trasladar al alto ejecutivo a los lugares más lejanos y a la mayor velocidad, el modelo cuenta con un potente motor Pratt & Whitney que le garantiza una autonomía de más de 3.000 millas náuticas. De hecho, su estabilidad y su rendimiento en vuelo han llevado a un buen número de pilotos a reconocer que "no han pilotado un aparato mejor". Su diseño, obra de Honeywell Primus EPIC, ha creado la cabina más amplia de todos los *jets* de su gama y garantiza la comodidad del cuarto de baño, al igual que espacio más que suficiente para equipaje y mercancías. Raytheon Aircraft ofrece al propietario la posibilidad de configurar el interior a su gusto, tanto en el número y colocación de los asientos como en la tapicería y los acabados en madera. El sistema electrónico de entretenimiento Collins Airshow contribuye a hacer del vuelo una experiencia divertida, tranquila y agradable.

Décrit à juste titre par ses créateurs comme étant le « jet privé de taille moyenne le plus luxueux du monde », le Hawker 4000 est le nouveau fleuron de Raytheon Aircraft. Conçu pour transporter un cadre supérieur vers les destinations les plus éloignées et le plus rapidement possible, le modèle est doté d'un puissant moteur Pratt & Whitney qui garantit une autonomie supérieure à 3 000 miles nautiques. Par conséquent, sa stabilité et son rendement en vol ont amené un grand nombre de pilotes à reconnaître qu'ils « n'ont jamais piloté de meilleur appareil ». Son design, signé Honeywell Primus EPIC, a permis de concevoir la cabine la plus spacieuse de tous les jets de sa catégorie, et propose également le confort d'une salle de bain ainsi qu'un espace plus que suffisant pour le rangement des bagages et des marchandises. Par ailleurs, Raytheon Aircraft offre au propriétaire la possibilité d'aménager l'intérieur selon ses goûts : il peut choisir le nombre et l'emplacement des sièges, les garnitures intérieures et les finitions en bois. Le système électronique de distraction Collins Airshow contribue à faire du vol une expérience divertissante, reposante et agréable.

TECHNICAL SPECIFICATIONS

Manufacturer	Raytheon Aircraft
Price	On request
Contact	www.hawkerbeechcraft.com
Type	Super-midsize Business Jet
Passenger capacity	2+8/14
Engines	2 x Pratt & Whitney PW308A
Range	3,200 nm
Cruise speed	485 mph | 782 km/h
Max. cruise speed	541 mph | 870 km/h
Length	68.9 ft | 21.08 m
Height	16.4 ft | 5.97 m
Span	59 ft | 18.82 m
Baggage capacity	114.42 ft³ | 3.24 m³
Empty weight	22,473 lbs | 10,194 kg

BOEING BUSINESS JETS (BBJ 2)

The Boeing Business Jets (BBJ) is a high performance version of the 737-700 Next-Generation. Designed for business travel and VIPs, the BBJ 2 has the cabin dimensions of the 737-700 (110 ft) and uses the wing and landing gear from the longer range 737-800. This custom-made private business jet offers its owners a maximum reach of 7,135 miles. It is powered by the same engines as the commercial 737 Next-Generation airplanes. This jet flies at a speed of 541 mph and can serve such routes as Los Angeles-London, New York-Buenos Aires or London-Johannesburg. Furthermore, the BBJ 2 has three times more space than any other jet in its category and has a greater cargo capacity than any competing model. The BBJ and the BBJ 2 are unbeatable in terms of spaciousness, comfort and utility and have a worldwide support program with specialist services and representatives.

El Boeing Business Jets (BBJ) es una versión de alto rendimiento del 737-700 Next-Generation. Diseñado para actividades corporativas y vip, el BBJ combina el tamaño de fuselaje del 737-700 (33,6 m) con las alas reforzadas y el tren de aterrizaje del 737-800, un modelo más grande y pesado. Esta combinación, hecha a medida, proporciona a los propietarios un reactor de negocios que cuenta con un alcance máximo de 11.482 km. Este *jet* opera con los mismos motores que los aviones comerciales 737 Next-Generation. El avión vuela a una velocidad de 871 km/h y realiza rutas como Los Ángeles-Londres, Nueva York-Buenos Aires o Londres-Johannesburgo. El BBJ posee, además, tres veces más espacio que otros aviones de su categoría y ofrece una flexibilidad de carga mayor que cualquier otro competidor. El BBJ y el BBJ 2 son insuperables en cuanto a espacio, confort y utilidad, y cuentan con un programa de apoyo al producto con servicios especializados y representación en todo el mundo.

Le Boeing Jets Business (BBJ) est une version hautes performances du modèle 737-700 Next-Generation. Conçu pour des activités d'entreprises et VIP, le BBJ allie la taille du fuselage du 737-700 (33,6 mètres) avec les ailes renforcées et le train d'atterrissage du 737-800, un modèle plus grand et plus lourd. Cette combinaison sur mesure offre aux propriétaires un avion d'affaires doté d'une autonomie maximale de 5 199 milles nautiques. Ce jet est propulsé par les mêmes moteurs que ceux installés sur les avions commerciaux 737 Next-Generation. L'avion vole à une vitesse de 871 km/h et réalise des trajets comme Los Angeles-Londres, New York-Buenos Aires ou Londres-Johannesburg. Par ailleurs, les espaces du BBJ sont trois fois plus spacieux que ceux des autres avions de sa catégorie. Il offre ainsi une capacité de charge beaucoup plus importante que n'importe quel autre concurrent. En matière d'espace, de confort et de fonctionnalité, le BBJ et le BBJ 2 sont les premiers de leur catégorie. Ils sont dotés d'un programme d'assistance proposant des services spécialisés et une représentation dans le monde entier.

TECHNICAL SPECIFICATIONS

Manufacturer	Boeing
Price	On request
Contact	www.boeing.com
Type	Wide body jet airliner
Passenger capacity	Ranges between 8 and 47
Engines	CFM56-7B27/B3
Range	5,199 nm (25 passengers)
Cruise speed	530 mph | 853 km/h
Max. cruise speed	541 mph | 871 km/h
Length	110.24 ft | 33.6 m
Height	41.2 ft | 12.5 m (tail height)
Wingspan	117.4 ft | 35.8 m
Baggage capacity	N.I.
Empty weight	103,220 lb | 46,820 kg

GULFSTREAM G500

The G500 has the best cabin space of any airplane in its class. It has three different interior designs to choose from, and four very different lounge spaces. For its size, power and flexibility, the G500 is the world's most renowned private jet for business trips. It has comfortable rest spaces, bedrooms, meeting spaces and bathrooms with showers. Furthermore, it has a fully equipped kitchen offering the best culinary services. Its stylish and comfortable cabin boasts DVD players, two LCD screens and a wireless Internet connection, amongst other facilities. The G500 has a temperature control system that pumps 100% fresh air and can be controlled from different points in the passenger cabin. The G500 has low noise levels, and extra soundproofing can be added upon request. The G500 can carry between 14 and 19 passengers. It has a non-stop flight time of 14 hours. Its sensor system means it can land in spaces that other jets cannot.

El G500 dispone de la mejor cabina en su categoría y ofrece tres diseños distintos de interior y cuatro zonas de estar bien diferenciadas. Por su tamaño, potencia y flexibilidad, el G500 es el reactor privado más apreciado del mundo para viajes de negocios. Posee cómodas áreas de descanso, dormitorios, zonas de reunión y baños con cabinas de ducha. Además, cuenta con una cocina perfectamente equipada para ofrecer los mejores servicios. Su elegante y confortable cabina está equipada con dos pantallas LCD, reproductores de DVD y *router* inalámbrico, entre otros servicios. Presenta un sistema de control de la temperatura que proporciona aire fresco y puede controlarse desde distintos puntos de la cabina de pasajeros. Los niveles de ruido en cabina son muy bajos, pudiéndose además instalar nuevos aislamientos a petición del cliente. El G500 tiene capacidad para transportar entre 14 y 19 personas y puede volar más de 14 horas sin repostar. Además, su sistema de sensores le permite aterrizar en lugares donde otros *jets* privados no podrían hacerlo.

Le G500 est équipé de la meilleure cabine de sa catégorie et offre trois conceptions d'intérieur différentes, ainsi que quatre zones de séjour totalement séparées. En raison de sa taille, de sa puissance et de sa polyvalence, le G500 est l'avion privé le plus apprécié du monde pour les voyages d'affaires. Il possède des espaces de repos confortables, des chambres à coucher, des zones de réunion et des salles de bains équipées de cabines de douche. De plus, une cuisine parfaitement équipée a été intégrée pour offrir les meilleurs services. Son élégante et confortable cabine est équipée de deux écrans LCD, de lecteurs DVD, d'un router Wifi et d'autres services. Il présente également un système de contrôle de température, qui donne de l'air frais et qui peut se réguler depuis différents points de la cabine des passagers. Le niveau sonore en cabine est très faible et des isolations supplémentaires peuvent être installées à la demande du client. Le G500 peut accueillir entre 14 et 19 personnes et voler plus de 14 heures sans escale. Par ailleurs, son système de capteurs lui permet d'atterrir dans des lieux où d'autres jets privés ne pourraient le faire.

TECHNICAL SPECIFICATIONS

Manufacturer	Gulfstream
Price	€ 28,859,000
Contact	www.gulfstream.com
Type	Business jet
Passenger capacity	14-19
Engines	2 x Rolls-Royce BR710
Range	5,800 nm
Cruise speed	528 mph | 850 km/h
Max. cruise speed	550 mph | 885 km/h
Length	96.4 ft | 29.4 m
Height	25.8 ft | 7.9 m
Wingspan	93.5 ft | 28.5 m
Baggage capacity	226 ft³ | 6.4 m³
Empty weight	54,500 lb | 24,721 kg

CESSNA CITATION X

With a maximum cruise speed of Mach 0.92, Cessna's best equipped model is the fastest private jet in history. It is capable of flying just under the speed of sound and has a moderate fuel consumption (in fact it consumes less fuel than some slower jets). This allows it to fly for up to 3,402 nautical miles without refueling, at an average height of 43,000 ft. Its cabin is designed to offer maximum comfort. There is room for nine passengers with the standard equipment and the corridor has a height of 5.6 ft, high enough for an adult to stand up without bending over too much. The Citation X is capable of flying from New York to Los Angeles in less than four hours and is the ideal private jet for a Top Executive who needs to arrive in the shortest possible time and in the most comfortable manner. The golf player Arnold Palmer and the Formula 1 champion Nelson Piquet are just two of its owners.

Con una velocidad máxima de crucero de Mach 0,92, el modelo mejor equipado de la marca Cessna es el reactor privado más rápido de la historia. Un vuelo a una velocidad apenas unas décimas por debajo de la del sonido le permite, gracias también a su consumo moderado —de hecho consume menos combustible que algunos *jets* más lentos—, alcanzar una autonomía de hasta 3.402 millas náuticas, volando a una media de 13.000 m de altura. Su cabina está diseñada para brindar la máxima comodidad; con el equipamiento estándar hay espacio para nueve pasajeros y el pasillo mide 1,70 m, altura suficiente para que una persona se ponga de pie sin tener que inclinarse demasiado. Capaz de llevarnos de Nueva York a Los Ángeles en menos de cuatro horas, el Citation X es el reactor privado ideal para el alto ejecutivo que quiera llegar en el menor tiempo posible y viajar de la manera más cómoda. El golfista Arnold Palmer y el campeón de Fórmula 1 Nelson Piquet ya figuran entre sus propietarios.

Avec une vitesse de croisière maximale de Mach 0,92, le modèle le mieux équipé de la marque Cessna est l'avion privé le plus rapide de l'histoire. Grâce à sa faible consommation et en volant à une vitesse légèrement inférieure à celle du son et à 13 000 m d'altitude en moyenne, cet avion peut d'atteindre une autonomie de 3 402 milles nautiques. Sa cabine a été conçue pour offrir un confort optimal ; avec l'équipement standard, il est possible d'accueillir neuf passagers. Le couloir, d'une hauteur de 1,70 m, permet de se tenir debout sans devoir trop se pencher. Capable de relier New York à Los Angeles en moins de quatre heures, le Citation X est l'avion privé idéal pour un cadre supérieur qui souhaiterait arriver à destination le plus vite possible tout en bénéficiant du meilleur confort. Le joueur de golf Arnold Palmer et le champion de Formule 1 Nelson Piquet figurent parmi la liste des propriétaires de cet avion.

TECHNICAL SPECIFICATIONS

Manufacturer	Cessna Aircraft Company
Price	€ 14,644,000
Contact	www.citationx.cessna.com
Type	Medium-sized business jet
Passenger capacity	12
Engines	2 x Rolls-Royce AE 3007C turbofans
Range	3,070 mi | 5,686 km with 36,100 lb | 16,375 kg
Cruise speed	Mach 0.90
Max. cruise speed	Mach 0.92
Length	72.18 ft | 22 m
Height	18.93 ft | 5.77 m
Span	63.91 ft | 19.48 m
Baggage capacity	81.22 ft³ | 2.30 m³
Empty weight	21,450.98 lbs | 9,730 kg

GULFSTREAM G550

The Gulfstream G550 is one of its maker's insignia jets. Its features make it the perfect jet for long distance flights. The G550 flies 6,750 nautical miles from New York to Tokyo, even with headwinds. It flies further, and more quickly than any of the other private jets in its category. It is also the most versatile model and is capable of carrying up to eight passengers from coast to coast in the United States on one single tank of fuel. Great height, extreme heat, short runways, strong headwinds... are no match for this superb machine. The craftsmanship of the Gulfstream engineers has combined turbo reactor Rolls-Royce BR710 engines with aerodynamic advances. This has achieved outstanding results, such as its non stop reach which has been increased to an amazing 6,750 nautical miles at Mach 0.80. Gulfstream guarantees 24 hour technical assistance 365 days of the year. The sophisticated cabin has a high level of comfort; seats can be joined and adapted to meet the needs of long distance journeys, in which travelers need to work or even sleep.

Gulfstream G550 es uno de los aviones insignia de la flota de la empresa. Sus características lo hacen perfecto para vuelos de largo recorrido. El G550 recorre 6.750 millas náuticas desde Nueva York hasta Tokio incluso con vientos en contra; vuela más lejos y más rápido que cualquiera de los aviones privados de su categoría. Este modelo es también el más versátil y es capaz de llevar a ocho pasajeros de una costa a la otra de los Estados Unidos con un solo depósito. Gran altitud, calor extremo, pistas cortas, fuertes vientos en contra... ninguna de estas circunstancias supone un problema para este magnífico aparato. El trabajo de los ingenieros de Gulfstream ha combinado los motores turborreactores Rolls-Royce BR710 con importantes mejoras en lo que a la aerodinámica respecta. De este modo, se han conseguido resultados extraordinarios, como la ampliación de su autonomía para no repostar hasta unas increíbles 6.750 millas náuticas a Mach 0,80. Gulfstream garantiza, además, soporte técnico 24 horas al día, los 365 días del año. La sofisticación de la cabina va acompañada de un elevado confort; los asientos se pueden agrupar y ajustar para satisfacer las necesidades de los viajes largos en los que es necesario trabajar o incluso dormir.

Gulfstream G550 est l'un des avions insignes de la flotte de l'entreprise. Ses caractéristiques le rendent parfait pour des vols de longue distance. Le G550 assure un vol de 6 750 milles marins de New York à Tokyo, même avec un vent contraire; il vole plus loin et plus vite que n'importe lequel des avions privés de sa catégorie. Ce modèle est aussi le plus polyvalent et il est capable de transporter huit passagers d'une côte des États-Unis à l'autre sans escale. Grande altitude, chaleur extrême, pistes courtes, vents contraires forts... aucune de ces circonstances ne pose de problème à ce magnifique appareil. Les ingénieurs de Gulfstream ont combiné les moteurs turboréacteurs Rolls-Royce BR710 avec des améliorations dans l'aérodynamique, obtenant des résultats extraordinaires, tels que l'augmentation de son autonomie pour ne pas faire d'escale jusqu'aux incroyables 6 750 milles marins à Mach 0,80. Gulfstream garantit en outre une assistance technique 24 heures sur 24, 365 jours par an. La sophistication de la cabine est accompagnée d'un confort élevé; les sièges peuvent être regroupés et ajustés pour s'adapter aux besoins de voyages longs au cours desquels il est nécessaire de travailler ou même de dormir.

TECHNICAL SPECIFICATIONS

Manufacturer	Gulfstream
Price	€ 34,689,000
Contact	www.gulfstream.com
Type	Light-midsize business jet
Passenger capacity	14-18
Engines	2 x Rolls-Royce BR710
Range	6,750 nm at Mach 0.80
Cruise speed	Mach 0.85
Max. Cruise speed	Mach 0.885
Length	96.42 ft | 29.4 m
Height	25.83 ft | 7.9 m
Wingspan	93.5 ft | 28.5 m
Baggage capacity	226 ft³ | 6.4 m³
Empty weight	48,300 lb | 21,909 kg

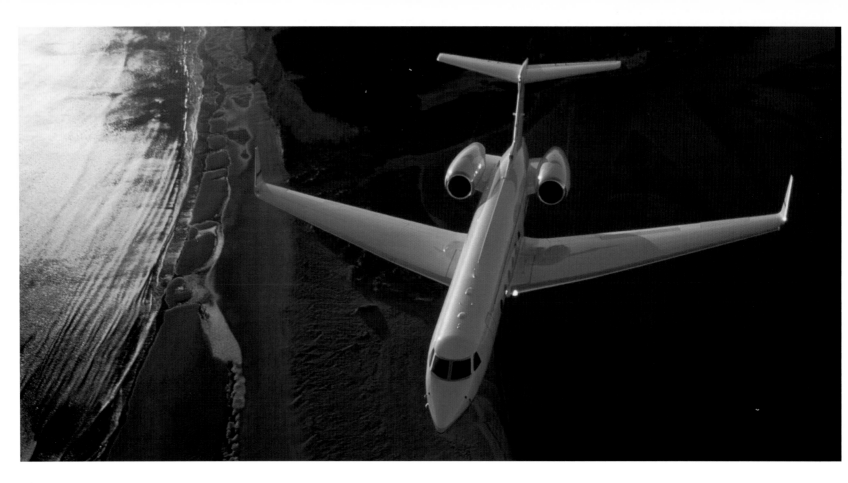

CESSNA MUSTANG

Cessna broke into the growing market of light jets with the creation of the Mustang model. Built by the Cessna group II design development program, this business jet has four seats for passengers and can easily be piloted by its owner. With a non-stop flight capacity of 1,240 miles, it is the ideal private jet for passengers who do not need to cover intercontinental distances, although the two Pratt & Whitney PW615F engines give it the necessary power to reach the not inconsiderable top speed record of 506.5 miles/hour. Its reduced cabin is an example of good use of space, with four armchairs facing each other in pairs to guarantee enough seating room for the occupants. The interior design offers a variety of upholstery and lining options, and the four chairs, a sofa and a bathroom come as standard.

Con el nacimiento del modelo Mustang, la casa Cessna se estrenó en el creciente mercado de los *jets* ligeros. Construido por el programa de desarrollo de diseño Cessna grupo II, este reactor de negocios cuenta con cuatro plazas para pasajeros y no plantea dificultades para ser pilotado incluso por su propietario. Con una autonomía de más de 2.000 km, es el *jet* privado ideal para un viajero que no precise cubrir distancias intercontinentales, aunque sus dos motores Pratt & Whitney PW615F le otorgan la potencia necesaria para alcanzar la nada desdeñable marca de 815 km/h de velocidad punta. Su reducida cabina es un ejemplo de aprovechamiento del espacio, con cuatro sillones enfrentados por parejas con el fin de garantizar espacio suficiente para los ocupantes que tomen asiento. El diseño de los interiores permite elegir entre diferentes opciones de tapicería y revestimientos, y el equipamiento básico consiste en esos cuatro asientos, un sofá y un baño.

Avec la création du modèle Mustang, l'entreprise Cessna se lance pour la première fois sur le marché en plein essor des jets légers. Construit grâce au programme de développement du design de Cessna grupo II, cet avion d'affaires peut accueillir quatre passagers et être piloté sans aucune difficulté par son propriétaire. Avec une autonomie de plus de 2 000 km, ce jet privé est idéal pour le voyageur qui ne recherche pas à parcourir des milliers de kilomètres, bien que ses deux moteurs Pratt & Whitney PW615F lui confèrent la puissance nécessaire pour atteindre une vitesse de pointe de 815 km/h. Sa petite cabine illustre parfaitement l'optimisation de l'espace, avec quatre fauteuils disposés face à face, garantissant un espace suffisant pour les occupants qui y prennent place. Le design intérieur permet de choisir entre différentes options de housses et de revêtements : l'équipement standard comprend quatre sièges, un canapé et une salle de bain.

TECHNICAL SPECIFICATIONS

Manufacturer	Cessna Aircraft Company
Price	€ 1,892,000
Contact	www.mustang.cessna.com
Type	Super light business jet
Passenger capacity	4
Engines	2 Pratt & Whitney Canada PW615F
Range	1,150 nm
Cruise speed	374.69 mph	603 km/h
Max. cruise speed	506.42 mph	815 km/h
Length	38.91 ft	11.86 m
Height	13.75 ft	4.19 m
Span	42.22 ft	12.87 m
Baggage capacity	44.85 ft³	1.27 m³
Empty weight	N.I.

AMERICAN EUROCOPTER VIP EC 155 B1

This elegant and slender helicopter combines excellent performance with a smooth and silent piloting. Its cabin is much more spacious than the cabins of other helicopters in its category. The EC 155 B1 model has strengthened two very important aspects of this mode of transport: speed and passenger comfort. The technological advances, such as the Spheriflex five blade main rotor and the Fenestron tail rotor, have minimized vibrations at high speed. This model is marketed as the helicopter for VIPs, companies and public services. The pilot's cabin includes the latest advances and is ergonomically designed to make piloting a real pleasure. It is available in different versions, its deluxe, attractive and elegant interior seats up to 8 passengers. The seats are spacious armchairs that ensure the greatest of comfort on all routes. Summing up, the VIP EC 155 B1 marks a new way of flying first class.

Este elegante y esbelto helicóptero combina un excelente rendimiento con un pilotaje suave y silencioso. Posee una cabina mucho más amplia que la disponible en otros helicópteros de su clase. En el modelo EC 155 B1 se han potenciado dos aspectos muy importantes en este tipo de transporte: la velocidad y el confort de los pasajeros. Los avances tecnológicos, como el rotor principal de cinco palas Spheriflex y el rotor de cola Fenestron, han conseguido reducir las vibraciones cuando se vuela a gran velocidad. Este modelo aspira a ser el helicóptero para vips, empresas y servicios públicos. La cabina de los pilotos incorpora los últimos avances tecnológicos y está ergonómicamente diseñada para que pilotar este aparato sea un verdadero placer. Disponible en varias versiones, su lujoso interior tiene capacidad para ocho pasajeros y goza de un diseño refinado y atractivo. Los asientos son amplios sillones que aseguran una gran comodidad en todos los trayectos. En resumen, el VIP EC 155 B1 define una nueva manera de volar en primera clase.

Cet hélicoptère élégant et svelte allie un excellent rendement avec un pilotage doux et silencieux. Il possède une cabine beaucoup plus spacieuse que celle d'autres hélicoptères de sa catégorie. Dans ce modèle EC 155 B1, on a amélioré deux aspects très importants de ce type de transport : la vitesse et le confort des passagers. Les progrès technologiques, avec le rotor principal à cinq pales Spheriflex et le rotor de queue Fenestron, ont réussi à réduire les vibrations à grande vitesse. Ce modèle aspire à être l'hélicoptère des VIPS, des entreprises et des services publics. La cabine des pilotes est équipée des dernières nouveautés et elle est ergonomiquement conçue pour que piloter cet appareil soit un véritable plaisir. Disponible en plusieurs versions, son intérieur luxueux offre des sièges à huit passagers et un design raffiné et attrayant. Les sièges sont de vastes fauteuils qui assurent un grand confort pour tous les trajets. En définitive, le VIP EC 155 B1 représente une nouvelle manière de voler en première classe.

TECHNICAL SPECIFICATIONS

Manufacturer	American Eurocopter
Price	€ 5,801,219
Contact	www.eurocopter.com
Type	Medium-twin helicopter
Passenger capacity	8
Enginés	2 x 935 shp turboshaft
Range	457 nm
Cruise speed	167.77 mph | 270 km/h at 6,000 ft | 1,829 m
Max. cruise speed	183.93 mph | 296 km/h
Length	41.70 ft | 12.71 m
Height	14.27 ft | 4.35 m
Wingspan	41.34 ft | 12.60 m
Baggage capacity	N.I.
Empty weight	5,774 lb | 2,619 kg

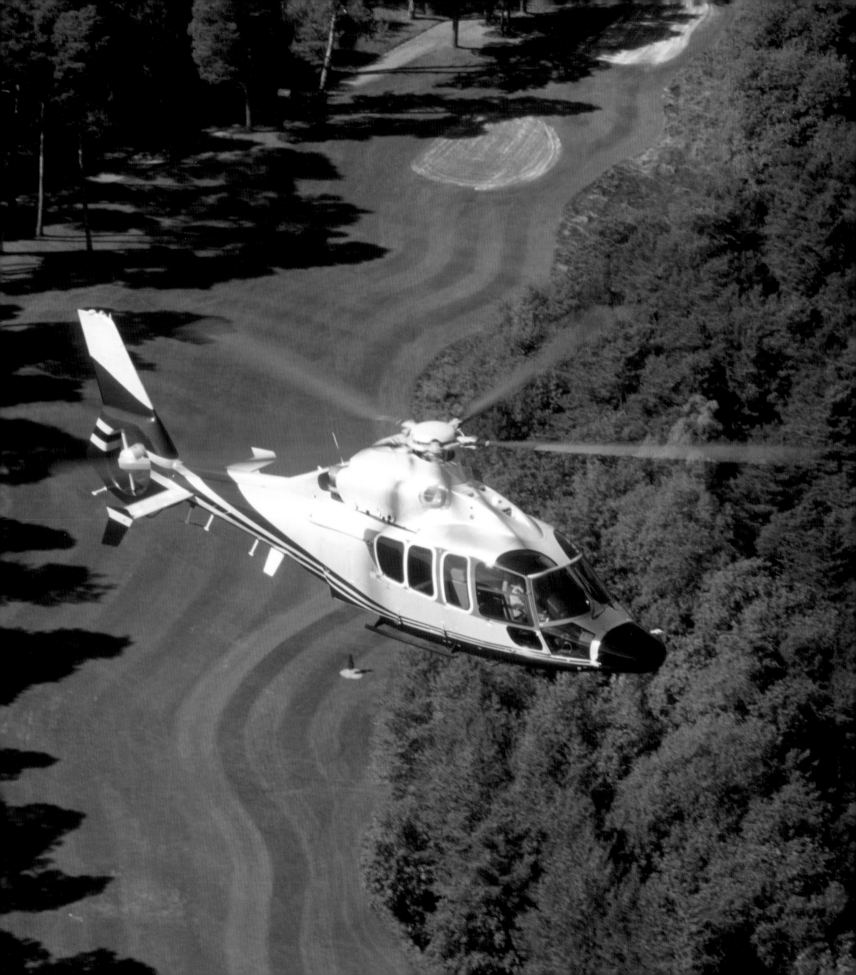

AGUSTA WESTLAND GRAND

The Grand helicopter is a new machine designed to meet the needs of the market. The Grand model is a breakthrough for the industry. Until it appeared on the market only larger helicopters had such a spacious interior. The Grand has the latest advances in technology and safety, eg., crash resistant fuel tanks, duplicated main systems and an ergonomic cockpit with high visibility to help piloting. The passenger cabin is a comfortable and peaceful space which is remarkably elegant, with a high level of soundproofing. Naturally, the interior design can be adjusted to the owner's needs and personal taste. Mention should be made of the large luggage area and the two spacious movable doors that allow easy access to the cabin interior.

El helicóptero Grand es un nuevo aparato desarrollado para satisfacer las necesidades del mercado. El modelo Grand supone un gran avance en el sector, pues hasta su aparición sólo los helicópteros de mayores dimensiones gozaban de una amplitud y un espacio interior similares. Cuenta con los últimos avances en términos de tecnología y seguridad, como por ejemplo depósitos de combustible resistentes a impactos, sistemas centrales duplicados o una cabina de mando ergonómica y con gran visibilidad para facilitar el pilotaje. La cabina de pasajeros, que presume de ser extremadamente elegante y de tener un gran aislamiento acústico, proporciona un entorno confortable y tranquilo. El diseño interior puede, por supuesto, adaptarse a las necesidades y gustos de cada propietario y destaca por su gran compartimento para el equipaje y las dos amplias puertas correderas que permiten un acceso fácil al interior de la cabina.

L'hélicoptère Grand est un nouvel appareil fabriqué pour satisfaire les besoins du marché. Le modèle Grand suppose un progrès important dans le secteur, car jusqu'à son apparition, seuls les hélicoptères de grandes dimensions disposaient d'un espace intérieur similaire. Il dispose des derniers progrès dans le domaine de la technologie et de la sécurité, par exemple des réservoirs de combustible résistants aux chocs, des systèmes centraux doubles ou une cabine de commande ergonomique dotée d'une grande visibilité pour faciliter le pilotage. La cabine des passagers, extrêmement élégante et qui offre une grande isolation acoustique, apporte une ambiance confortable et tranquille. Le design intérieur peut, bien sûr, s'adapter aux besoins et aux goûts de chaque propriétaire et se distingue par son grand compartiment réservé aux bagages et les deux grandes portes coulissantes qui permettent un accès facile à l'intérieur de la cabine.

TECHNICAL SPECIFICATIONS

Manufacturer	Agusta Westland
Price	On request
Contact	www.agustawestland.com
Type	Light twin helicopter
Passenger capacity	6
Engines	2 x Pratt & Whitney PW207C turboshaft
Range	295 nm (3-cell fuel system) / 432 nm (5-cell fuel system)
Cruise speed	155.34 mph | 250 km/h
Max. cruise speed	178.33 mph | 287 km/h
Length	42.5 ft | 12.96 m
Height	11.2 ft | 3.44 m
Width	25.5 ft | 7.76 m
Baggage capacity	N.I.
Empty weight	3,649 lb | 1,655 kg

AGUSTA WESTLAND A109 POWER

For many years, Agusta Westland has been the leading manufacturer of helicopters for executives and VIPs. It has sold models to more than 80 countries worldwide. Since its appearance on the market, the A109 POWER has met the needs of clients in both the private and business sectors. This helicopter has eight comfortable seats, and combines safety features with some impressive operational features, such as a maximum cruising speed at 177 mph. As well as being cost efficient, it is elegant, high-speed, productive and flexible thus making it a powerful and trustworthy vehicle. This helicopter can be made according to the needs of each user, who can choose between different features including: the engine, some additional communication features and naturally—the passenger cabin layout.

Desde hace muchos años Agusta Westland es la empresa líder en el sector de la fabricación de helicópteros para ejecutivos y personalidades vip. Sus modelos son vendidos en más de 80 países de todo el mundo. Desde su aparición, el modelo A109 POWER ha podido satisfacer las necesidades de los clientes, ya sea para el uso privado, ya para el empresarial. Este helicóptero posee ocho confortables plazas y combina elementos de seguridad con unas magníficas características operacionales, como la velocidad máxima de crucero de 285 km/h. A la eficiencia de los costes se le añaden la elegancia, la alta velocidad, la gran productividad y la flexibilidad para ofrecer un vehículo potente y fiable. Este helicóptero puede construirse en función de las necesidades de cada usuario, el cual puede elegir varios de sus elementos. Entre éstos se encuentran el motor, algunos elementos de comunicación adicionales y, por supuesto, la configuración del interior de la cabina de pasajeros.

Depuis de longues années, Agusta Westland est l'entreprise leader dans le secteur de la fabrication d'hélicoptères pour cadres supérieurs et personnalités VIP. Ils ont fourni leurs modèles à plus de 80 pays du monde entier. Depuis son apparition, le modèle A109 POWER a pu satisfaire les besoins des clients, pour un usage privé ou d'entreprise. Cet hélicoptère possède huit places confortables et combine des éléments de sécurité avec de magnifiques caractéristiques opérationnelles, telles que la vitesse maximale de croisière de 285 km/h. Il faut ajouter à l'efficacité des coûts l'élégance, la vitesse élevée, la grande productivité et la flexibilité pour proposer un véhicule puissant et fiable. Cet hélicoptère peut être construit en fonction des besoins de chaque usager qui choisit plusieurs de ses éléments. Parmi ceux-ci se trouvent le moteur, quelques éléments de communication supplémentaires et, bien sûr, la configuration de l'intérieur de la cabine des passagers.

TECHNICAL SPECIFICATIONS

Manufacturer	Agusta Westland
Price	On request
Contact	www.agustawestland.com
Type	Light twin turbine helicopter
Passenger capacity	8
Engines	2 x Pratt & Whitney PW206C
Range	512 nm
Cruise speed	N.I.
Max. cruise speed	177 mph	285 km/h
Length	37.59 ft	11.45 m
Height	11.48 ft	3.50 m
Wingspan	36 ft	11 m
Baggage capacity	N.I.
Empty weight	3,494 lb	1,585 kg

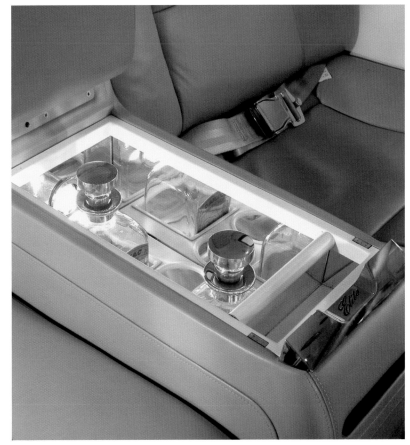

AGUSTA WESTLAND AW 139

The AW139 is the new benchmark helicopter for executives. It has been designed to meet the needs of the most discerning travelers, and surpasses all other helicopters in its class in terms of capability, speed, ride quality and passenger cabin space. The AW139 marks the standard for deluxe interiors, with minimal noise and vibration levels and most importantly—high power. Its performance is outstanding and is guaranteed in flights across the world, and in extreme weather conditions. This machine has a spacious cabin which can house travelers in great comfort. The flexibility of its design means that the seat layout can be changed to make the most of the views from its six large windows. Special mention should be made of its ability to ascend and descend, and easy access to the luggage compartment from the inside.

El AW139 es el nuevo helicóptero de referencia para ejecutivos. Se ha diseñado para satisfacer las necesidades de los viajeros más exigentes; supera al resto de los helicópteros de su tipo en capacidad, velocidad, calidad de pilotaje y amplitud de la cabina de pasajeros. El AW139 define el estándar de lo que debe ser un interior de lujo, unos niveles de ruido y vibración bajos y, sobre todo, una gran potencia. Su rendimiento es excepcional y está garantizado en vuelos en todo el mundo, incluso en las condiciones ambientales más extremas. Este aparato posee una cabina muy amplia donde acomodar con gran confort a los viajeros. La flexibilidad de su diseño permite cambiar la configuración de los asientos y proporcionar vistas a través de sus seis grandes ventanas. También cabe destacar la facilidad para ascender y descender del helicóptero y el acceso directo, desde el interior, al compartimento de equipaje.

L'AW139 est le nouvel hélicoptère de référence pour cadres supérieurs. On l'a conçu pour satisfaire les besoins des voyageurs les plus exigeants ; il dépasse le reste des hélicoptères de sa catégorie en capacité, vitesse, qualité de pilotage et ampleur de la cabine de passagers. L'AW139 définit les standards de l'intérieur de luxe, des niveaux de bruit et de vibrations bas, et surtout, de la puissance. Ses performances sont exceptionnelles et assurent des vols dans le monde entier, même dans les conditions les plus extrêmes. Cet appareil possède une cabine très spacieuse où peuvent s'installer très confortablement les voyageurs. La variabilité de son design permet de changer la configuration des sièges afin que tous les passagers puissent voir à travers ses six grandes fenêtres. Il convient aussi de souligner l'aisance avec laquelle on peut monter et descendre de l'hélicoptère et l'accès facile, depuis l'intérieur, au compartiment des bagages.

TECHNICAL SPECIFICATIONS

Manufacturer	Agusta Westland
Price	On request
Contact	www.agustawestland.com
Type	Medium twin-engine helicopter
Passenger capacity	6-8
Engines	2 x Pratt & Whitney PT6C-67C turboshafts with FADEC
Range	573 nm
Cruise speed	190 mph	306 km/h
Max. cruise speed	N.I.
Length	54.66 ft	16.66 m
Height	16.24 ft	4.95 m
Wingspan	45.28 ft	13.8 m
Baggage capacity	120 ft³	3.4 m³
Typical equipped weight	8,509 lb	3,860 kg

Luxury destinations

Destinos de lujo

Destinations de luxe

Luxury destinations
Destinos de lujo
Destinations de luxe

The mere possession of riches does not guarantee a life of luxury and splendor if wealth and status is not used to enjoy exclusive holidays far away from mass tourism destinations. Opulent lifestyles are synonymous with escaping from the day-to-day routine to faraway places, pampering oneself and enjoying peaceful moments with the very best attention and service. Private islands, exclusive spas, remote hideaways and heavenly spots by the sea are much sought-after for relaxation and to experience fabulous sensations. Very few people are able to travel to wherever they chose on the planet, and disappear for a while. It is a real luxury that only a small part of the population can afford, and which is envied by the rest of us simple mortals who can only dream of such places. This chapter presents some of the most extraordinary places where spectacular, exotic landscapes, sophisticated atmospheres or relaxation treatments may be enjoyed and memories may be treasured ever after. These hideaways offer exotic food, adventure sports and endless activities. The selection of establishments for this book includes an impressive holistic spa in Bhutan, New York's most exclusive hotel and the world's only 7 star hotel, located in the city of Dubai.

Una vida de lujo y de esplendor no significa sólo poseer riquezas, sino también tener un estatus y un nivel económico que permita disfrutar de vacaciones exclusivas lejos de los destinos turísticos más habituales. Vivir en la opulencia significa escapar de la rutina para refugiarse en lugares lejanos; significa también dejarse cuidar y disfrutar de momentos de descanso y de las mejores atenciones y servicios. Las islas privadas, los *spas* exclusivos, los refugios recónditos o algún paraíso junto al mar son lo que el hombre puede desear para relajarse y experimentar sensaciones maravillosas. La posibilidad de escoger viajar a cualquier lugar, a cualquier punto del planeta, para abandonar la vida diaria es una elección al alcance de muy pocos, un verdadero lujo del que disfruta una pequeñísima parte de la población, por supuesto envidiada por los demás simples mortales que sólo en su imaginación pueden visitar estos sitios. En este capítulo se presentan algunos de los lugares más excepcionales donde se puede gozar de paisajes impresionantes y exóticos, de ambientes sofisticados o simplemente de tratamientos de relax que quedarán para siempre en la memoria. En estos *resorts* se disfruta de comidas exóticas, de deportes de aventuras y de un sinfín de actividades. La selección de establecimientos para este libro incluye un impresionante *spa* holístico en Bhután, el hotel más distinguido de Nueva York y el único hotel de siete estrellas del mundo, situado en la ciudad de Dubai.

Une vie de luxe et de splendeur, ce n'est pas seulement à posséder des richesses, mais jouir d'un statut social et d'un niveau économique élevé, qui permet de profiter de vacances exceptionnelles, loin des destinations touristiques les plus fréquentées. Vivre dans l'opulence et l'abondance permet de s'échapper vers des lieux éloignés pour fuir la routine, mais aussi de se laisser choyer et de profiter de moments de détente et des meilleures attentions et services. Les îles privées, les meilleurs spas, les refuges retirés ou un petit coin de paradis en bord de mer représentent tout ce que peut désirer un homme pour se reposer et connaître des sensations merveilleuses. Pouvoir voyager vers n'importe quel point de la planète afin de disparaître un moment, n'est pas à la portée de tous. En fait il s'agit d'un véritable luxe dont ne profite qu'une infime partie de la population, évidemment jalousée par le commun des mortels, qui ne peut visiter ces lieux qu'en rêve. Ce chapitre présente quelques-unes de ces destinations où il est possible de profiter de paysages impressionnants, d'environnements sophistiqués ou simplement de soins relaxants inoubliables. Dans ces complexes, les clients peuvent goûter à des plats exotiques, s'adonner aux sports d'aventure et à une multitude d'activités. Un impressionnant spa holistique au Bhoutan, l'hôtel le plus chic de New York et l'unique hôtel sept étoiles du monde, situé à Dubaï, ont été sélectionnés pour réaliser ce livre.

VILLA AMISTÀ LEADING HOTELS OF THE WORLD

This charming palace is found in the land of Romeo and Juliet, surrounded by the vineyards used to elaborate one of the most exquisite Italian wines, the Valpolicella. The hotel is flanked by a beautiful garden, of more than 215,278 ft^2 with infinite hidden corners where one can breathe in the peace and quiet. There is also a cosmetic and well-being center in the hotel that offers various services to guests, from aromatherapy massages to aesthetic cures, mud baths, hydrotherapy and color therapy. In Villa Amistà history blends with the modernity of its interior design and with the numerous works of art that make this place a true contemporary art gallery. The rooms are decorated in an eclectic style that blends Baroque style with modern design and the latest technology. A prestigious gourmet restaurant for creative cuisine and the now legendary Peter's bar, with its vivacious and modern atmosphere, completes the services of this exclusive hotel with a unique personality.

En la tierra de Romeo y Julieta y rodeado de campos de cultivo dedicado a la producción de uno de los más exquisitos vinos italianos, el Valpolicella, se encuentra este encantador palacio. El hotel está flanqueado por un jardín bellísimo, de más de 20.000 m^2, con infinidad de rincones secretos y donde se respira una gran tranquilidad. El hotel alberga, además, un centro de cosmética y bienestar que ofrece servicios variados a los huéspedes, desde aromaterapia hasta curas estéticas, baños de barro, hidroterapia y cromoterapia. En Villa Amistà la historia se funde con la contemporaneidad de sus interiores y con las numerosas obras de arte que hacen de este lugar un verdadero museo de arte contemporáneo. Las habitaciones están decoradas con un estilo ecléctico que combina a la perfección el barroco con el diseño actual y las últimas tecnologías. Un prestigioso restaurante *gourmet* de cocina creativa y el ya legendario Peter's Bar, de atmósfera efervescente y moderna, completan los servicios de este exclusivo hotel de personalidad única.

Ce palais enchanteur se trouve sur les terres de Roméo et Juliette, au cœur des vignes réservées à la production du Valpolicella, l'un des vins italiens les plus exquis. L'hôtel est entouré d'un magnifique jardin de plus de 20 000 m^2, avec une infinité de petits recoins secrets où l'on peut jouir d'une grande tranquillité. L'hôtel accueille également un institut de beauté et de bien être, qui offre des soins variés aux clients : massages d'aromathérapie, cures esthétiques, bains de boue, hydrothérapie et chromothérapie. Dans l'hôtel Villa Amistà, l'histoire se fond avec la modernité de la décoration intérieure et avec les nombreuses œuvres d'art qui font de ce lieu un véritable musée d'art contemporain. Les chambres présentent un style éclectique, combinant à la perfection le baroque et le design actuel, et offrent les technologies les plus avancées. Un prestigieux restaurant *gourmet* où l'on peut goûter une cuisine créative ainsi que le légendaire Peter's bar, doté d'une atmosphère moderne et chaleureuse, complètent les services de ce merveilleux hôtel, unique en son genre.

SPECIFICATIONS

Name	Villa Amistà
Group	Leading Hotels of the World
Location	Verona, Italy
Architect/designer	Alessandro Mendini over an 18th century villa
No. rooms	60
Prices	Suites from € 330 to € 1,100
Special features	An authentic Neoclassical Venetian villa redesigned with a refreshingly innovative style
Contact	www.byblosarthotel.com

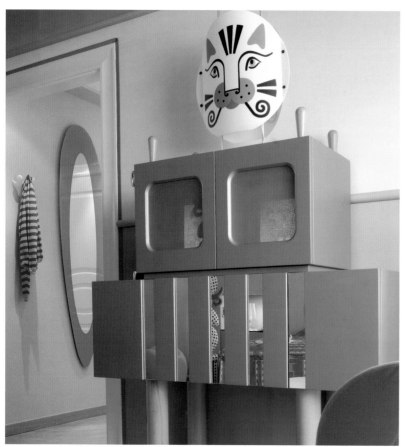

BURJ AL ARAB JUMEIRAH

The Burj Al Arab is considered the most luxurious hotel in the world and it is the only one with a seven star rating. It has 202 duplex suites ranging from 1,830 to 8,400 ft². Each one has an exclusive guest service and a personal butler, and with fully-equipped office services as well as independent dining and living rooms. The bathrooms have a spa and Jacuzzi where guests are pampered with music and aromatherapy prepared by the personal butler. The outstanding Assawan Spa, located in the communal area on the 18th floor, has spectacular views over the Persian Gulf, offers treatments such as hydrotherapy baths and oriental massages, and has solariums, a sauna, Turkish baths, two swimming pools and two fully-equipped fitness rooms. The Majles Al Bahar private beach can be reached directly from the hotel. The reception rooms have extraordinary dimensions and breath-taking elegance. The hotel chefs run a catering service in the reception areas, and the hotel's eight restaurants and lounges offer the most varied and exquisite culinary specialties.

El Burj Al Arab está considerado el hotel más lujoso del mundo, el único que posee siete estrellas. Dispone de 202 *suites* dúplex con espacios que van desde los 170 hasta los 780 m². Cada una de ellas cuenta en exclusiva con su propio servicio de huéspedes y de mayordomo. Junto con el comedor y la sala de estar independientes, cada *suite* dispone de servicios de oficina completos. En los baños, un *spa* y un *jacuzzi* esperan a todos los huéspedes, donde son agasajados con un menú de baño con música y aromaterapia preparado por el mayordomo personal. En los espacios comunes, el maravilloso Spa Assawan situado en el piso 18, con espectaculares vistas al golfo Pérsico, incluye desde hidroterapia, masaje oriental, solariums, sauna y baños turcos hasta dos piscinas y dos salas de *fitness* completamente equipadas. Además, desde el hotel se puede acceder libremente a la playa privada de Majles Al Bahar. En las salas de recepción, de dimensiones excepcionales y asombrosa elegancia, se ofrece un servicio de *catering*, a cargo de los mismos chefs del hotel, que dispone, además, de ocho restaurantes y *lounges* que ofrecen las más variadas y exquisitas especialidades culinarias.

L'hôtel Burj Al Arab, considéré comme l'hôtel le plus luxueux du monde, est le seul à posséder sept étoiles. Il comprend 202 suites duplex d'une superficie allant de 170 à 780 m². À chaque suite correspondent un majordome et un service d'étage exclusif. En plus d'une salle à manger et d'un séjour indépendants, chacune d'elles est équipée pour permettre à ses clients de travailler. Dans chaque salle de bain, les clients, choyés avec de la musique, peuvent profiter d'un spa et d'un jacuzzi, ainsi que de divers soins comprenant l'aromathérapie, préparés par le majordome. Dans les parties communes, situé au 18ème étage et jouissant d'un magnifique panorama sur le golfe Persique, le merveilleux Spa Assawan propose divers soins : bains d'hydrothérapie, massages orientaux, solariums, saunas, bains turcs, ainsi que deux piscines et deux salles de remise en forme, complètement équipées. De plus, les clients peuvent accéder librement à la plage privée de Majles Al Bahar depuis l'hôtel. Dans les salles de réception, exceptionnellement spacieuses et d'une élégance à couper le souffle, le service est assuré par les chefs cuisiniers des huit restaurants et *lounges* que compte l'hôtel, offrant aux clients les spécialités culinaires les plus variées et les plus exquises.

SPECIFICATIONS

Name	Burj Al Arab
Group	Jumeirah
Location	Dubai
No. rooms	202
Prices	From € 1,520
Special features	The only hotel in the world with a 7-star unofficial category
Contact	www.burj-al-arab.com

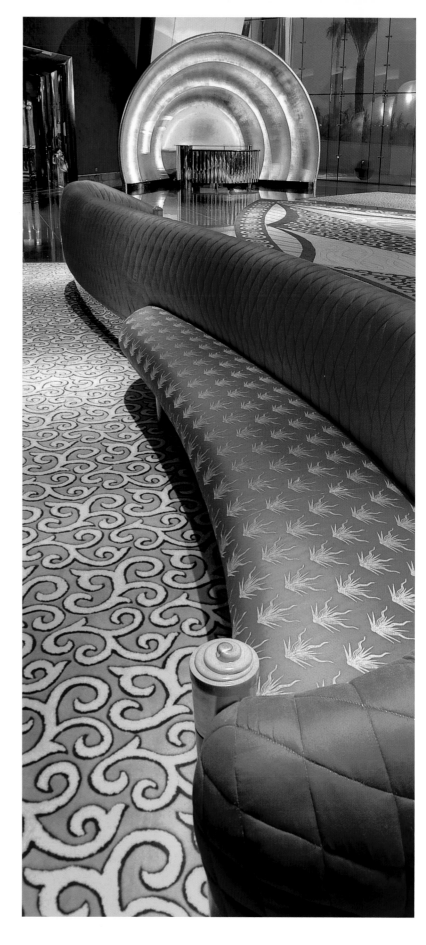

BULGARI RESORT BULGARI HOTELS AND RESORTS

Standing 525 ft above the Indian Ocean is one of the most exclusive and exotic hideaways in the world. The overwhelming natural beauty of this isolated spot is complemented perfectly by Bulgari's undisputed design. Three key elements define this idyllic place: its unique location; the combination of traditional Bali style with daring Italian contemporary design; and a variety of services that further emphasize the quality of the space and the comfort of the guests. Hand-cut volcanic rock, exotic wood and exquisite upholstery have been used in the construction and decoration of the hotel. A spectacular combination of original island materials is combined with an incredible collection of Balinese antiquities. The ornaments that decorate all the spaces have been designed by a team of local artists in collaboration with the architects. Each one of the private villas has a pool and a small tropical garden that enjoys total intimacy. Exclusive facilities include restaurants with Balinese and Italian specialties, the lounge bar, the spa and the pool cut into the cliffs. It is crowned by an impressive Hindu temple, in line with the island's religious tradition.

A 160 m sobre el océano Índico, se levanta uno de los refugios más exclusivos y exóticos del mundo. La sobrecogedora belleza natural de este enclave apartado se complementa de un modo ideal con el inigualable diseño Bulgari. Los tres elementos clave que definen este lugar idílico son su localización única, la mezcla del estilo tradicional de la isla de Bali con el atrevido diseño contemporáneo italiano, y una variedad de servicios en la que se priman la calidad del espacio y el confort de sus huéspedes. En la construcción del hotel se han empleado piedra volcánica tallada a mano, maderas exóticas y tapicerías exquisitas. Una espectacular mezcla de materiales originales de la isla se combina con una colección increíble de antigüedades balinesas. Los ornamentos que decoran todos los espacios han sido diseñados por un equipo de artistas locales en colaboración con los arquitectos. Cada una de las villas privadas tiene una piscina y un pequeño jardín tropical que goza de absoluta privacidad. Restaurantes con especialidades balinesas e italianas, un *lounge* bar, un *spa* y una piscina situada junto al acantilado son algunas de las exclusivas instalaciones de este lugar, coronado por un impresionante templo hindú dedicado al cultotradicional de la isla.

A 160 mètres au-dessus de l'océan Indien, se dresse l'un des refuges les plus exclusifs et les plus exotiques du monde. La saisissante beauté naturelle de cette enclave est en parfaite harmonie avec le design inégalable de Bulgari. Trois éléments essentiels définissent ce petit coin de paradis : sa situation unique, le mélange du style traditionnel balinais avec le design italien contemporain et audacieux, et la variété des services privilégiant la qualité de l'espace et le confort des hôtes. Pour la construction de cet hôtel, des pierres volcaniques taillées à la main, des bois exotiques et de somptueuses étoffes ont été utilisés : un mariage spectaculaire de matériaux originaires de l'île associés à une collection incroyable d'antiquités balinaises. Les ornements qui décorent toutes les pièces ont été conçus par une équipe d'artistes locaux en collaboration avec les architectes. Chaque villa privée comprend une piscine et un petit jardin tropical, qui jouit d'une parfaite intimité. Les restaurants proposent des spécialités balinaises et italiennes. En plus du *lounge bar*, le spa et la piscine située à côté de la falaise, font partie intégrante des installations uniques de ce lieu, dominé par un impressionnant temple hindou, consacré au culte traditionnel dans l'île.

SPECIFICATIONS

Name	Bulgari Resort
Group	Bulgari Hotels and Resorts
Location	Pecatu, Bali
Architect/designer	Antonio Citterio
No. rooms	59 bedroom villas with ocean view; 3 two-bedroom villas; the 14,000 ft² | 1,300 m² Villa Bulgari
Prices	From € 815 to € 3,700
Special features	A nearly 1 mile long beach, reached only via the resort's inclined lift
Contact	www.bulgarihotels.com

UMA PARO   COMO SHAMBHALA

The small and sheltered Buddhist kingdom of Bhutan, located in the Himalayan mountain range has only recently opened to foreign visitors. The Como Shambala refuge is located on a mountain peak at an altitude of 7,550 ft. It is one of the most exquisite holistic spas in the world and has been built to blend in with the philosophy of its surroundings. A privileged place has been chosen in the natural surroundings for its facilities, which include the mystical open-air yoga pavilion with breathtaking views over the Paro valley: pine forests, fields, small villages, rivers that flow down the mountainsides, and peaks hidden in the clouds. The height of the refuge is extremely beneficial for blood pressure, weight can be lost more easily and the quality of sleep is improved notably. Besides the exquisite indoor spaces and the sports and leisure facilities, the hotel organizes exclusive tours, mountain biking, and visits to Bhutan's impressive temples. A perfect complement for health treatments and a genuine holistic experience.

Situado en plena cordillera del Himalaya, el pequeño y resguardado reino budista de Bhután se ha abierto muy recientemente al visitante extranjero. El refugio de Como Shambala, situado a 2.300 m de altitud en lo alto de un colina, es uno de los *spas* holísticos más exquisitos del mundo, cuya concepción armoniza con la filosofía del entorno. Para sus instalaciones se ha elegido un lugar privilegiado del maravilloso paisaje circundante, como, por ejemplo, en el caso del mágico pabellón de yoga al aire libre que goza de espectaculares vistas al valle de Paro: bosques de pinos, campos, pequeños poblados y ríos que descienden entre las montañas rodeadas de nubes. La altura a la que se sitúa el refugio es altamente beneficiosa para la presión sanguínea, lo que permite perder peso con mayor facilidad y mejora notablemente el sueño. Además de los exquisitos espacios interiores y de las instalaciones deportivas y de relax, el hotel ofrece rutas exclusivas, ciclismo de montaña y visitas a los impresionantes templos del país. Un complemento perfecto para los tratamientos de salud y una auténtica experiencia holística.

Situé au cœur des hauts-plateaux de l'Himalaya, le petit royaume bouddhiste du Bhoutan s'est très récemment ouvert aux visiteurs étrangers. Le refuge de Como Shambala, situé à 2 300 m d'altitude, au sommet d'une colline, est l'un des spas holistiques les plus agréables au monde, conçu en totale harmonie avec la philosophie du lieu qui l'entoure. Des endroits exquis au cœur d'un paysage somptueux ont été choisis pour accueillir ses différentes installations, comme le féerique pavillon à ciel ouvert réservé au yoga, qui jouit d'un panorama spectaculaire sur la vallée de Paro : forêts de pins, champs, hameaux et rivières descendant des montagnes entourées de nuages. L'altitude à laquelle se situe le refuge est très bénéfique pour la tension, ce qui permet de perdre plus facilement du poids et d'améliorer nettement la qualité du sommeil. En plus des fabuleux intérieurs et des installations consacrées aux activités sportives et à la relaxation, l'hôtel propose des randonnées uniques, la visite des plus beaux temples du pays et la possibilité de faire du cyclisme de montagne. Toutes ces activités complètent parfaitement les soins de santé et l'authentique expérience holistique proposés tout au long du séjour.

SPECIFICATIONS

Name	Uma Paro
Group	Como Shambhala
Location	Paro, Bhutan
No. rooms	20 rooms and 9 villas
Prices	Suites from € 890; villas from € 1,185
Special features	Constructed on a mountain top, this refuge is devised as a place for rest, meditation and relaxation
Contact	www.comoshambhala.bz

CASA TRITÓN

Casa Tritón is located in one of the most elegant and exclusive holiday spots on the Pacific. It is a private villa but with all the comforts and privileged spaces of a five star hotel. A complete service team composed of nine assistants takes cares of every detail and oversees the organization of activities within and outside the house. The best chef in the area manages the kitchen and pampers the guests with the most exquisite Mexican nouvelle cuisine seafood dishes. Careyes is one of the most important natural parks in Mexico, and various species of exotic birds can be spotted from Casa Tritón, as well as whales, pods of dolphins, and even giant sea turtles. The house is surrounded by an exotic garden and built 395 ft above sea level. It enjoys incomparable views over the Pacific Ocean and is considered an architectural masterpiece, with indoor spaces open on three sides and totally lacking in glass. The windows are closed by means of wooden shutters and the interiors blend with the landscape. Each one of the suites is an independent bungalow.

Situada en uno de los lugares vacacionales del Pacífico más elegantes y exclusivos, Casa Tritón es una villa particular pero con el confort y el espacio privilegiado propios de un hotel de cinco estrellas. Un equipo de servicio compuesto por nueve asistentes cuida de todos los detalles y se encarga de la organización de actividades dentro y fuera de la casa. La mejor chef del lugar dirige la cocina y agasaja a los huéspedes con exquisitos platos de la *nouvelle cuisine* mexicana, especializada en marisco. Careyes es uno de los oasis naturales más importantes de México, y desde Casa Tritón se puede contemplar las más variadas especies de aves exóticas, así como ballenas, bancos de delfines e incluso tortugas gigantes. La casa está rodeada por un exótico jardín y construida a 120 m sobre el nivel del mar. Disfruta de unas vistas panorámicas inigualables del océano Pacífico y está considerada una obra maestra de la arquitectura, con espacios interiores abiertos en tres lados y sin cristal. Las ventanas se cierran mediante persianas de madera; los interiores se funden con el paisaje. Cada una de sus *suites* constituye un *bungalow* independiente.

Située dans l'une des enclaves les plus élégantes et somptueuses de l'océan Pacifique, la Casa Tritón est une villa particulière, dotée de tout le confort nécessaire et d'espaces privilégiés similaires à ceux d'un hôtel cinq étoiles. Neuf assistants veillent à ce que tout soit parfait et assurent l'organisation des différentes activités à l'intérieur et à l'extérieur de la maison. Le meilleur chef est aux fourneaux et choie ses hôtes en leur préparant les plats les plus exquis de la *nouvelle cuisine* mexicaine, spécialisée en fruits de mer. Careyes est l'une des réserves naturelles les plus importantes du Mexique. Depuis la Casa Tritón, il est possible de contempler différentes espèces d'oiseaux exotiques, ainsi que des baleines, des bancs de dauphins et même des tortues géantes. La villa, construite à 120 mètres au-dessus du niveau de la mer, est entourée d'un jardin exotique. Ses espaces intérieurs ouverts sur trois côtés et dépourvus de vitres, lui permettent de jouir des plus beaux panoramas sur l'océan Pacifique et font d'elle une œuvre d'art architecturale. Les fenêtres se ferment grâce à un système de persiennes en bois et l'intérieur fusionne avec le paysage. Chaque suite constitue un bungalow indépendant.

SPECIFICATIONS

Name	Casa Tritón
Location	Careyes, Puerto Vallarta, Mexico
Architect/designer	Marco Aldaco
No. rooms	3 + 3 in the guests' pavilion
Prices	From € 3,335 to € 5,190 per night
Special features	The architect Marco Aldaco camped for various weeks on this cliff top in order to determine the best layout and orientation of the house
Contact	www.casatriton.com

W Retreat and Spa Maldives
W Hotels

W Retreat and Spa is undoubtedly the paradigm of heaven on earth. Tucked away in one of the most beautiful spots on earth, it is the perfect place to combine treatments and activities in surroundings characterized by water, white sand and silence. The hotel has 78 independent villas, each one with its own private terrace and pool. One can opt for either an absolutely private ocean haven built over the water, or two-story villas beside the beach, or two-roomed villas with private pool at the water's edge. The elements blend with the natural surroundings; the roofs allow contemplation of the sky and the crystal floors reveal the lagoon fauna. Six restaurants each with a different atmosphere offer a variety of gastronomic choices of local specialties, interpreted in a modern and sophisticated manner, or with a simple style and rustic touches. The bar, where one can enjoy the most exquisite cocktails, is found in the center of the island, 50 ft below sea level. Activities include scuba diving, water sports and yoga sessions on the beach.

W Retreat and Spa Maldives es sin duda el paradigma del paraíso en la tierra. Situado en uno de los más bellos parajes del planeta, es el lugar perfecto para combinar tratamientos y diversión en un entorno dominado por el agua, las arenas blancas y el silencio. El hotel está compuesto por 78 villas independientes, cada una con terraza y piscina propias. Se puede elegir entre un alojamiento-isla construido sobre el agua y con privacidad absoluta, villas de dos niveles junto a la playa o villas de dos habitaciones con piscina muy cerca del mar. Los distintos elementos se funden gracias a las aberturas de los techos que permiten observar el cielo y a los suelos de cristal a través de los cuales puede admirarse la fauna de la laguna. La oferta gastronómica procede de seis restaurantes de distintos ambientes en los que se puede disfrutar de las especialidades locales interpretadas de forma moderna y sofisticada, o bien con un estilo sencillo y un toque rústico. El bar, en el que degustar los cócteles más exquisitos, se encuentra en el centro de la isla, a 15 m bajo el nivel del mar. Las actividades incluyen submarinismo, deportes náuticos y sesiones de yoga en la playa.

Le W Retreat et Spa est sans aucun doute le paradigme du paradis sur terre. Situé au cœur de l'un des plus beaux paysages du monde, ce lieu est parfait pour combiner remise en forme et divertissement, dans un environnement entouré d'eau, de plages de sable blanc et baigné de silence. L'hôtel comprend 78 villas indépendantes, toutes dotées d'une terrasse et d'une piscine. Le client peut choisir entre une maison sur pilotis au-dessus de l'eau et jouissant d'une intimité absolue, une villa à deux niveaux au bord de la plage, ou bien encore une villa aménagée avec deux chambres et une piscine face à la mer. Le design intérieur fusionne avec le paysage grâce aux ouvertures sur le ciel et aux sols en verre permettant d'observer la faune du lagon. L'hôtel comprend six restaurants aux différentes ambiances, où vous pourrez découvrir les interprétations modernes et sophistiquées des spécialités locales, ou bien une cuisine simple et rustique. Le bar, situé au centre de l'île, à 15 mètres au-dessous du niveau de la mer, propose les cocktails les plus exquis. Les activités proposées permettent de s'adonner aux plaisirs de la plongée sous-marine, des sports nautiques ou du yoga sur la plage.

SPECIFICATIONS

Name	W Retreat and Spa Maldives
Group	W Hotels
Location	Fesdu Island, North Ari Atoll, Maldives
No. rooms	78 villas each with private pool
Prices	Villas from € 740 to € 1,850 per night
Special features	A private island where style flirts with soul in a wonderland of white-sand beaches, turquoise lagoons and breathtaking reefs
Contact	www.starwoodhotels.com

GRAMERCY PARK HOTEL · IAN SCHRAGER

Guests and visitors to the Gramercy Park Hotel will find themselves in an unexpected and magical place. It reflects a new 21st century Bohemian style, a unique style created by the fusion of the minds of creative thinkers such as Julian Schnabel or Maarten Baas. The idiosyncrasy of its spaces and its eclecticism are based on an elegance lacking in conventionalisms, although it is inspired in the colors used by Renaissance painters such as Titian and Rafael in their works of art. All the hotel's details are synonymous with personality. It is an original, romantic, unexpected, poetic and whimsical place. Like a work of art, it inspires an emotional response in the visitor. Each one of its rooms and suites is unique, both in terms of structure and in terms of decoration, complemented by splendid pieces of art, especially selected for each space, hand-made carpets, carpets imported from all over the world, and rich velvet tapestries; the wood and the finishes contribute towards creating a lavish atmosphere. A myriad of cultures and styles is reflected in this timeless, eclectic and ultramodern mosaic.

El huésped o el visitante del Gramercy Park Hotel se encuentra inmerso en un ambiente sorprendente y mágico, un espíritu bohemio reinventado para el siglo XIX, un estilo único conseguido mediante la unión de mentes creativas como Julian Schnabel y Maarten Baas. La idiosincrasia y el eclecticismo de sus espacios se han logrado a través de una elegancia carente de convencionalismos, que, sin embargo, se inspira en la paleta de colores presente en las obras de pintores del Renacimiento como Tiziano y Rafael. Cada detalle de este hotel es sinónimo de personalidad. Es un espacio original, romántico, sorprendente, poético y caprichoso. Como una obra de arte, suscita una respuesta emocional en el visitante. Cada una de sus habitaciones y *suites* es única, tanto en su estructura como en la decoración, complementada por espléndidas piezas de arte seleccionadas especialmente para cada espacio, alfombras elaboradas a mano e importadas de distintos lugares del mundo, y ricas tapicerías de terciopelo; las maderas de los acabados contribuyen a crear un ambiente de gran confort. Una miríada de culturas y estilos se refleja en este mosaico intemporal, ecléctico y ultramoderno.

Le client ou visiteur du Gramercy Park Hotel se retrouve immergé dans un univers enchanteur et surprenant : la bohème réinventée pour le XXIᵉ siècle avec un style unique, grâce à l'association de talents créatifs comme ceux de Julian Schnabel et Maarten Baas. Le caractère personnel de ses espaces et son éclectisme sont le fruit d'une élégance dépourvue de tout conventionnalisme, s'inspirant cependant de la palette des peintres de la Renaissance tels Raphaël ou le Titien. Chaque détail de cet hôtel a sa personnalité. Cet espace, surprenant et fantaisiste, se distingue par son originalité, son romantisme et sa poésie. Comme le fait une œuvre d'art, il suscite une vive émotion dans le cœur de chaque visiteur. De par sa structure et sa décoration, chaque chambre, chaque suite est unique. Leur décoration est complétée par de splendides œuvres d'art choisies spécialement pour chacun des espaces : les tapis faits main et importés du monde entier, les magnifiques tapisseries de velours et le bois des finitions contribuent à créer un environnement des plus confortables. Une multitude de cultures et de styles se reflète dans cette mosaïque intemporelle, éclectique et ultramoderne.

SPECIFICATIONS

Name	Gramercy Park Hotel
Group	Ian Schrager
Location	New York, USA
Architect/designer	Michael Overington & Anda Andei
No. rooms	185
Prices	Suites from € 720 to € 2,965
Special features	The new flagship, a creation by the inimitable Ian Schrager, is a sensuous experience of artful diversity
Contact	www.gramercyparkhotel.com

STEAMWORKS

The Steamworks space was conceived with the intention of creating a bathing house with an exclusive variety of services for the gay community of Toronto. The architects drafted the idea of this space as an ideal and self-sufficient gay city. Steamworks is a deluxe and elegant sanctuary for clients, to forget about daily stress and keep their privacy. The program includes 75 changing areas, a gym, treatment cabins, two lounges, a DJ box, humid and dry saunas and two pools at different temperatures. The spaces are aimed towards easing socialization and relaxation. The breakthrough style of these baths is based on original solutions that successfully accentuate physical and visual contact. The two lounges work as meeting centers where visitors may socialize in comfort. The design is a contrast for the senses, with warm and cold elements that juxtapose so that the guests can show themselves off without feeling discomfort. It is a space of great exclusivity and comfort that has been converted into a refuge from the standards that prevail outside its walls.

Steamworks fue concebido como una casa de baños con una exclusiva variedad de servicios para la comunidad gay de Toronto. Los arquitectos dibujaron la idea de este espacio como una ciudad gay, ideal y autosuficiente. Steamworks pretende ser un santuario de gran lujo y elegancia para los clientes en el que evadirse y olvidar el estrés diario y preservar su privacidad. El programa incluye 75 espacios de vestuario, gimnasio, cabinas de tratamiento, dos *lounges*, una cabina de DJ, saunas húmedas y secas, y dos bañeras a distintas temperaturas. Los espacios están pensados para facilitar la socialización y el relax. El estilo rompedor de estos baños se basa en originales soluciones que consiguen realzar el contacto físico y visual. Los dos *lounges* actúan como centros de encuentro en los que los visitantes pueden socializarse con comodidad. El diseño es un contraste para los sentidos, con elementos cálidos y fríos que se yuxtaponen para que los huéspedes puedan exhibirse y estar protegidos a la vez. Un espacio de gran exclusividad y confort que se ha convertido en un refugio de las normas imperantes en el exterior.

L'espace Steamworks a été conçu dans le but de créer une maison de bains proposant une multitude de services exclusifs à la communauté gay de Toronto. Les architectes envisageaient une ville gay, idéale et autosuffisante. Steamworks se présente comme un sanctuaire très luxueux et élégant, où les clients peuvent s'évader, oublier le stress quotidien et préserver leur intimité. Réparti en 75 pièces, ce lieu comprend des vestiaires, une salle de sport, des cabines de soins, deux *lounges*, une cabine de DJ, des saunas secs et humides, des hammams et deux bassins à différentes températures. Ces espaces facilitent le repos et le contact social. Le style singulier des salles de bain repose sur des solutions originales, qui créent un contact physique et visuel. Les deux *lounges* fonctionnent comme des espaces de rencontre où les visiteurs peuvent faire connaissance tout en bénéficiant d'un grand confort. Le design de ce lieu est caractérisé par un jeu de contrastes pour les sens : des éléments chauds et froids se superposent pour que les clients puissent se montrer tout en restant protégés. Le Steamworks est un espace très luxueux et confortable qui s'est transformé en refuge, loin des normes du monde extérieur.

SPECIFICATIONS

Name	Steamworks
Location	Toronto, Canada
Architect/designer	McIntosh Poris Associates
Prices	According to treatments
Special features	Inspired by the marketplaces of Pompey, a place in which to relax and socialize where the body-beautiful prevail
Contact	www.steamworksonline.com

DOLCE & GABBANA
BEAUTY FARM AND BAR MARTINI

Dolce and Gabbana, gurus from the world of fashion and design, have created an innovative transversal concept of leisure and care for men in a historic, late eighteenth century palace. It offers multiple possibilities, from buying a suit to total relax, from latest generation cosmetic treatments to a cocktail or a sophisticated and quick aperitif in the Bar Martini, which occupies two floors beside the Dolce & Gabbana Uomo boutique. The Beauty Farm is located in the inviting small square that is found in the interior of the shop. It is spectacularly modern and has the most advanced technologies in order to offer total comfort to men and women of any age. The bar was conceived by Ferruccio Laviani and has been totally designed in black, from the polished stone walls to the leather armchairs and coffee tables. A spectacular red dragon can be seen on the black mosaic floor tiles. An imposing chandelier made of Murano blown crystal and designed by Dolce & Gabbana, gleams in the center.

En un histórico palacio de finales del siglo XVIII, Dolce & Gabbana, grandes gurús de la moda y el diseño, han creado un innovador concepto transversal de ocio y cuidado para el hombre. Las posibilidades son múltiples: desde probarse un traje hasta disfrutar de un relax total, de tratamientos cosméticos de última generación, de un cóctel o de un sofisticado y veloz aperitivo en el Bar Martini, de dos plantas y situado junto a la *boutique* Dolce & Gabbana Uomo. Beauty Farm se encuentra en la sugestiva plazoleta que se abre en el interior de la tienda. Un espacio de modernidad espectacular que incorpora las tecnologías más avanzadas y ofrece un confort completo a hombres y mujeres de cualquier edad. El bar, concebido por Ferruccio Laviani, ha sido diseñado totalmente en negro, desde los muros de piedra pulida hasta los sillones de piel y las mesillas. En el mosaico de los pavimentos, también en negro, se puede observar un espectacular dragón rojo. Diseñada por Dolce & Gabbana, una imponente lámpara *chandelier* de cristal soplado de Murano resplandece en el centro de este espacio.

Dans cet authentique palais de la fin du XVIIIe siècle, Dolce et Gabbana, grands noms de la mode et du design, ont créé un concept transversal novateur de loisirs et de soins. Ce concept offre de multiples possibilités : le client peut s'offrir un costume ou une tenue décontractée, profiter des soins cosmétiques les plus récents de dernière génération, ou boire un cocktail et manger un amuse-gueule sophistiqué et rapidement servi au Bar martini, sur deux étages, à côté de la boutique Dolce & Gabbana Uomo. La Beauty Farm est située sur une séduisante petite place qui s'ouvre sur l'intérieur de la boutique. Cet espace, d'une modernité spectaculaire, intègre les technologies les plus avancées et offre tout le confort nécessaire aux hommes et femmes de tout âge. Le bar, conçu par Ferruccio Laviani, a été réalisé tout en noir, depuis les murs de pierre polie jusqu'aux sièges en cuir et les petites tables. Sur le sol en mosaïque, également noir, se déploie un spectaculaire dragon rouge. Une impressionnante lampe *chandelier* en verre soufflé de Murano, conçue par Dolce & Gabbana, resplendit au centre de cet espace.

SPECIFICATIONS

Name	Dolce & Gabbana Beauty Farm and Bar Martini
Location	Corso Venezia 15, Milan, Italy
Architect/designer	David Chipperfield, Ferrucio Laviani
Prices	According to treatment
Special features	Traditional methods are used to shave and trim beards in the timelessly elegant barbershop
Contact	www.dolcegabbana.it / tel.: +39 02 76 40 88 88

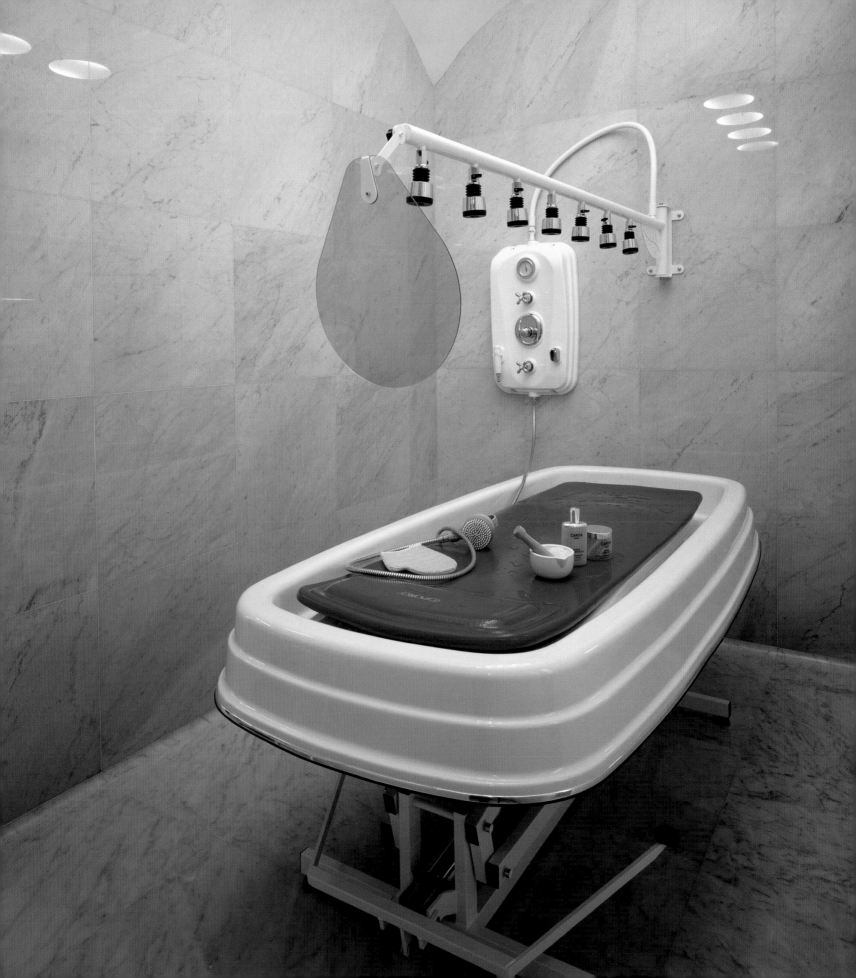

Luxury moments

Momentos de lujo

Instants de luxe

Luxury moments
Momentos de lujo
Instants de luxe

The real scope of luxury is hidden in details. For those who like to surround themselves with the luxuries of life, and for those who choose to indulge in just one aspect of their life, it is important to recognize exactly what it is that makes an object unique, that differentiates it from all others of its kind. This chapter does not merely include objects that give boundless pleasure to the owner. Rather, it includes objects that can be customized and made more personal. From the latest technology, to jewelry, accessories or the most exquisite gastronomic products, objects of various proportions are presented here that can be customized to order, and that can even be designed by the future owner. The section also includes articles produced in very limited series. Lovers of luxury, discerning consumers, and those who simply want to pamper themselves or give someone an unforgettable gift that only few people can afford, will discover a fascinating world in this section, the modern day equivalent to Ali Baba's mythical treasure cave. These valuable items that allure even the most discerning customers can be grouped into four different categories, in accordance with their functions.

El verdadero alcance del lujo reside realmente en los detalles. Tanto para quienes se rodean de los artículos más exclusivos como para quienes deciden colmar de suntuosidad un aspecto de su vida lo importante es reconocer y saber distinguir aquello que convierte a cualquier objeto en algo único, que lo diferencia de todos los demás de su especie. Por ello, en este capítulo se ha buscado incluir objetos que, además de otorgar el placer inconfundible de poseerlos, también permiten a sus propietarios darles un carácter único y personal que los haga más suyos. Desde la alta tecnología hasta las piezas de joyería, los accesorios o los productos gastronómicos más exquisitos, aquí se encuentran objetos de todas las dimensiones que se pueden personalizar por encargo, que incluso pueden ser casi diseñados por su futuro poseedor. La sección incluye también artículos fabricados en series limitadas muy reducidas. Los grandes sibaritas, los clientes más exigentes y aquellos que quieren regalarse o que desean obsequiar a alguien con los mejores productos, al alcance solamente de unos pocos, descubrirán en esta sección un mundo fascinante, el equivalente contemporáneo a los míticos tesoros de Alí Babá. Estos preciosos objetos se agrupan en cuatro clases según sus características y, por supuesto, harán las delicias hasta de los más exigentes.

La quintessence du luxe réside dans les détails. Pour les personnes qui s'entourent d'objets exclusifs ou qui décident de vouer au luxe un aspect de leur vie, l'important est de savoir distinguer ce qui peut transformer un objet anodin en un article unique, le différenciant des autres articles de sa catégorie. C'est pourquoi ce chapitre présente des objets qui, en plus de procurer un immense plaisir, confèrent à leurs propriétaires un caractère unique et personnel. De la haute technologie aux pièces de joaillerie, en passant par les accessoires ou les produits gastronomiques les plus succulents, ce chapitre décrit des objets de toutes tailles qui peuvent être personnalisés, voire conçus spécialement pour le futur acquéreur. Sont également présentés des articles fabriqués en série très limitée. Les grands sybarites, les clients les plus exigeants et les personnes qui aiment ou qui souhaitent offrir un produit exclusif, uniquement accessible à une élite, découvriront un monde fascinant : l'équivalent moderne de la caverne d'Ali Baba. Ces magnifiques objets sont regroupés en quatre types selon leurs caractéristiques, et, bien sûr, ils feront les délices des personnes les plus exigeantes.

MOMENTS OF SPORT

Sport is an ideal activity; it helps to keep us in shape and is beneficial to our health. As well as mental and physical benefits, sport provides moments of leisure when we can "switch off" from work and other commitments. The question that we must ask ourselves now is: What links luxury and sport? Sports that are linked to luxury require expensive equipment. Skiing, sailing and golf are obvious examples of this. However, aside from the materials and the manufacturers, there are certain features that mark the difference between the luxurious and the extraordinary. How many people have a sophisticated gym in their office? Or a custom-made bicycle?

El deporte es una actividad perfecta para divertirse; ayuda a mantener el cuerpo en forma y aporta múltiples beneficios para la salud. Además de todos estos beneficios de orden físico y psíquico, la práctica del deporte se asocia al esparcimiento, a los momentos de ocio y sobre todo a desconectar del trabajo y de las obligaciones. La pregunta que se plantea ahora es: ¿qué relación existe entre el lujo y el deporte? Los deportes que se asocian con el lujo acostumbran a necesitar un equipamiento de un coste más elevado. El esquí, la vela o el golf son claros ejemplos. Otros elementos, además de los materiales y los fabricantes escogidos, marcan la frontera de lo lujoso y extraordinario. ¿O es que disfrutar en el propio despacho de un aparato de gimnasia sofisticado o tener una bicicleta fabricada a medida está al alcance de cualquier persona?

Le sport est une activité de loisirs idéale; il aide à garder la forme physique et la santé. En plus de tous ces bénéfices sur le plan physique et psychique, la pratique du sport est associée à la distraction, à des moments de loisir et contribuent surtout à nous faire oublier un moment le travail et les obligations. La question que l'on se pose maintenant est : quelle relation existe-t-il entre luxe et sport ? Les sports associés au luxe requièrent habituellement un équipement plus coûteux. Le ski, la voile ou le golf le montrent clairement. D'autres éléments, en plus des matériaux et des fabricants choisis, marquent la frontière entre ce qui est luxueux et extraordinaire et ce qui ne l'est pas. Disposer dans son bureau d'un appareil de gymnastique sophistiqué ou avoir une bicyclette fabriquée sur mesure est-il à la portée de tout le monde ?

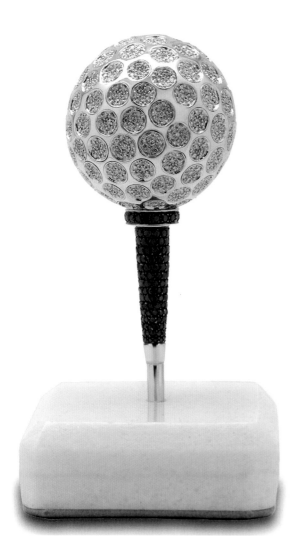

HR DIAMONDS   DIAMOND GOLF BALL

Designed by the renowned jeweler Bernard Marquin, exclusively for the Charles Hollander Collection, this lighter is an extremely valuable personal object for daily use, as well as a collectors' item. A unique object, manufactured in 18 karat gold and covered with 11 karat black diamonds.

Una realización exclusiva que será el regalo perfecto para cualquier amante del golf o del arte. Se presenta en un estuche lacado en negro que incluye una peana cubierta de diamantes negros. La pieza se ha fabricado en oro blanco de 18 quilates con diamantes blancos de 11 quilates engarzados.

Conçu exclusivement pour la collection Charles Hollander par le célèbre bijoutier Bernard Marquin, ce briquet est à la fois un objet personnel de grande valeur utilisable au quotidien et une pièce de collection. Une pièce unique, en or 18 carats, recouverte de diamants noirs de 11 carats.

SPECIFICATIONS

Design	Bernard Maquin
Contact	www.charleshollandercollection.com
Price	€ 18,300 approx.
Special Features	This exquisite example of high-quality jewelry has the exact shape of a golf ball

CALLAWAY GOLF
BIG BERTHA HEAVENWOOD HYBRIDS

Big Bertha is synonymous with the latest technological innovations in hybrids. It combines the performance and the sensation of long irons with the distance and forgiveness of woods. Designed to inspire confidence in your shots and create moments of inertia. The result offers a greater resistance to twisting, more stability and forgiveness.

Bigh Bertha es sinónimo de las últimas innovaciones tecnológicas en cuestión de híbridos. El rendimiento y la sensación de los hierros largos, unidos a la distancia de golpe y a la suavidad de las maderas, inspira confianza en los golpes y proporcionar maravillosos momentos de inercia. El resultado es una resistencia mayor a los giros y más estabilidad y soltura.

Le modèle Big Bertha est doté des dernières innovations technologiques en matière d'hybri-des. Les performances des fers longs s'unissent parfaitement à la distance et à la tolérance des différents bois. Il a été conçu pour donner pleinement confiance au golfeur au moment de la frappe et pour offrir de hauts moments d'inertie. Cela permet d'obtenir une meilleure résistance aux rotations, ainsi qu'une meilleure stabilité et plus d'aisance.

SPECIFICATIONS

Design	Callaway Golf
Contact	www.callawaygolf.com
Price	From € 330
Special features	Big Bertha is presented with seven different lofts to replace irons 1 to 7

CALLAWAY GOLF X-20 IRONS

The X-20 series has been created to offer serious golfers total performance with enhanced forgiveness. It is the ultimate in confidence and precision. The new X-20 irons deliver in every way by offering technology, innovation and playability that will take your game to a new level.

La serie X-20 se ha creado con todos los requisitos necesarios para satisfacer al golfista más exigente y ofrecerle un rendimiento total con una máxima suavidad de golpe. Se obtienen así una completa confianza y precisión. Los nuevos hierros X-20 reúnen la tecnología, la innovación y la flexibilidad que llevarán al jugador a un nivel superior.

La série X-20 a été fabriquée pour satisfaire les golfeurs les plus exigeants et leur offrir des performances optimales et une douceur de frappe maximale. Le joueur peut ainsi avoir une confiance absolue en ses capacités et d'une grande précision dans son jeu. Les nouveaux fers X-20 combinent technologie, innovation et souplesse, permettant au golfeur de passer au niveau supérieur.

SPECIFICATIONS

Design	Callaway Golf
Contact	www.callawaygolf.com
Price	From € 740
Special features	The X-20 series combines traditional style with Callaway Golf technology, resulting in maximum performance and confidence in playability

GREENWOOD GOLF CLUBS

These clubs are beautiful and durable, a treat for those who can afford the very best. They are made of three different woods, with silver finishes; each one is unique, with its own grain, as individual as a fingerprint. Currently, two heads are available: the mallet and the prism.

Un material para quienes pueden permitirse lo mejor, estos palos son bellos además de resistentes. Se presentan en tres maderas distintas, con acabados de plata y cada uno de ellos es único: tiene su propio grano, como si de una huella dactilar se tratara. Por el momento, están disponibles dos cabezas: *mallet* y *prism*.

Les personnes qui peuvent s'offrir ce qu'il y a de mieux, choisiront ces clubs de golf d'une exquise beauté et très résistants. Disponible en trois bois différents et doté de finitions en argent, chaque club est unique, avec son grain particulier aussi individuel qu'une empreinte digitale. Actuellement, deux têtes sont disponibles : l'une en forme de *maillet* et l'autre en forme de *prisme*.

SPECIFICATIONS

Design	Greenwood Golf Clubs
Contact	www.greenwoodgolf.com
Price	€ 1,030–€ 1,185/unit
Special features	These hand-crafted wooden putters are for the discerning player and collector who plans to hand them down to the younger generation

Serotta MeiVici

MeiVici is the first customized bicycle manufactured in carbon fiber and using aerospace technology. It is distinguished by its lightness, resistance and capacity to absorb vibrations. It is a unique article constructed to adapt to the driver's requirements regarding weight, size and specific use.

La primera bicicleta fabricada a medida mediante tecnología aeroespacial, completamente realizada en fibra de carbono, la MeiVici se distingue por su gran ligereza, resistencia y su capacidad de absorber las vibraciones. Un artículo único construido para adecuarse a los requerimientos de su conductor en cuanto a peso, tamaño y uso específico.

La MeiVici est la première bicyclette entièrement fabriquée en fibre de carbone et utilisant la technologie aérospatiale. Elle se distingue par sa grande légèreté, sa résistance et sa capacité à absorber les vibrations. Un article unique, construit pour s'adapter aux besoins de son conducteur en ce qui concerne son poids, sa taille et son utilisation spécifique.

SPECIFICATIONS

Design	Ben Serotta
Contact	www.serotta.com
Price	€ 8,200 approx.
Special features	Customized carbon fiber bicycle

CHANEL SKIS

Although Chanel is not a manufacturer of sporting material, who would doubt the quality of its products? The materials used by this exclusive brand name are the best to be found on the market and the production is subjected to high quality controls. With stylish and elegant lines, these skis are an example of class, distinction and of course, luxury.

Chanel no es un fabricante de material deportivo, es cierto, pero ¿quién pone en duda la calidad de sus productos? Los materiales que utiliza esta selecta marca son en cada caso los mejores y la producción sigue siempre unos altos controles de calidad. Las líneas estilizadas y elegantes hacen de estos esquís un ejemplo de clase, distinción y, por supuesto, de lujo.

Il est certain que Chanel n'est pas un équipementier sportif, mais qui peut remettre en cause la qualité de ses produits ? Les matériaux utilisés par cette luxueuse marque sont les meilleurs sur le marché et la production respecte toujours les contrôles de qualité les plus élevés. Les lignes stylisées et élégantes font de ces skis un exemple de classe, de distinction et bien évidemment de luxe.

SPECIFICATIONS

Design	Chanel
Contact	www.chanel.com
Price	On request
Special features	High-quality skis for exclusive clients who use exclusive, luxurious and glamorous products to stand out from the crowd

CHANEL FOOTBALL

There is no need to be a great sportsman or a football or rugby fan in order to appreciate this magnificent object. It is quite simply a marvel, a very desirable object. It can be purchased in some of the most select Chanel establishments, such as Jeffrey in New York or Maxfield in Los Angeles.

No hace falta ser un gran deportista, ni siquiera es necesario ser un aficionado al fútbol americano o al rugby para apreciar este magnífico objeto. La pieza es, por sí sola, una maravilla, un objeto de deseo. Se puede adquirir en algunos de los establecimientos Chanel más selectos, como el Jeffrey en Nueva York o el Maxfield, en Los Ángeles.

Il n'y a pas besoin d'être un grand sportif, ni un amateur de football américain ou de rugby pour apprécier ce magnifique objet. La pièce est à elle seule une merveille et un véritable objet de désir. Il peut être acheté dans les enseignes Chanel les plus sélectes, comme Jeffrey à New York ou Maxfield à Los Angeles.

SPECIFICATIONS

Design	Chanel
Contact	www.chanel.com
Price	€ 145
Special features	This original and fashionable ball is just one of the sporting articles lounched by this famous and prestigious company

YAMAHA FX CRUISER HO

This Yamaha jet ski is more comfortable and outperforms any other in its class. The model has various devices that make it really special. It has a 1,052 cc four cylinder, four-stroke engine. The steering column can be adjusted to the drivers preferred driving position. With a weight of 780 lbs it can carry up to three passengers.

El confort y el rendimiento de esta Yamaha son los mejores de su categoría. El modelo cuenta con varios dispositivos que lo hacen realmente especial. Su motor es de cuatro cilindros, con cuatro tiempos y 1.052 cc de potencia. Además, la altura del manillar es regulable para adaptarse al conductor. Con un peso de 354 kg, puede transportar hasta tres ocupantes.

Cette Yamaha est la plus confortable et la plus performante de sa catégorie. Le modèle intègre plusieurs dispositifs qui le rendent véritablement unique. Son moteur quatre cylindres quatre-temps a'une puissance de 1 052 cc. Par ailleurs, la hauteur du volant est réglable afin de s'adapter à chaque conducteur. Avec un poids de 354 kg, ce véhicule peut transporter jusqu'à trois passagers.

SPECIFICATIONS

Design	Yamaha
Contact	www.yamaha-motor.com/waverunner
Price	From € 8,320
Special features	This splendid jet ski has a special wide step for ease of boarding after a day of diving or a waterskiing session

WALLY SKIS

Wally designs and produces specialized skis with a carbon fiber structure based on the technology developed for their yachts. Each one of the models is devised for a determined use. The Tradition model, eg., is quick and has easy turning. The Wallypowder is a much wider ski, appropriate for off-piste.

Wally diseña y produce esquís muy especializados; su estructura de fibra de carbono está basada en la tecnología desarrollada para sus yates. Cada uno de los modelos está pensado para un uso determinado. El modelo Tradition, por ejemplo, es rápido y de giro fácil. El Wallypower es un esquí más ancho, adecuado para el esquí fuera de pista.

Wally dessine et fabrique des skis très spécialisés ; leur structure en fibre de carbone est basée sur la technologie développée pour les yachts de la marque. Chaque modèle est conçu pour un usage spécifique. Le modèle Tradition, par exemple, est rapide et permet de prendre les virages plus facilement, contrairement au Wallypower qui est un ski plus large et parfaitement adapté au hors-piste.

SPECIFICATIONS

Design	Wally
Contact	www.wally.com
Price	On request
Special features	Skis exclusively manufactured from carbon fiber with steel edges. The cores are made from birch, ash and poplar wood

TECHNOGYM   KINESIS PERSONAL

A product contemplated for spaces that are designed for people, such as: the home, innovative offices or exclusive hotel suites. The Kinesis Personal works all the body's muscular groups. Its versatility allows an infinite number of combinations by varying the operational position.

Un producto de diseño para espacios dedicados al cuidado personal y pensado tanto para utilizarlo en la casa como en las oficinas más innovadoras o en las *suites* de los hoteles más exclusivos. Con Kinesis Personal se pueden ejercitar todos los músculos del cuerpo. Su versatilidad permite infinitas combinaciones; para ello sólo hay que modificar la posición de trabajo.

Un produit de design conçu aussi bien pour la maison que pour les bureaux les plus innovateurs ou les suites des hôtels les plus élégants. Avec Kinesis Personal, on peut faire travailler tous les groupes musculaires du corps. Sa polyvalence permet des combinaisons infinies rien qu'en variant les réglages.

SPECIFICATIONS

Design	Antonio Citterio, Toan Nguyen
Contact	www.technogym.com
Price	From € 8,500
Special features	Inspired by nature and science. The Kinesis Personal uses the patented Fullgravity three-dimensional movement

TECHNOGYM CROSS FORMA

Cross Forma works the muscles in the legs and upper body in a way that burns more calories than any other exercise. Its special Long Stride feature guarantees ample movement during exercise, in an undeniably compact piece of equipment.

Cross Forma hace trabajar los músculos de las piernas y de la parte superior del cuerpo, de manera que permite alcanzar un consumo de calorías superior al de cualquier otro ejercicio. El especial mecanismo "Long Stride" garantiza la amplitud del movimiento durante el ejercicio, en un equipo indiscutiblemente compacto.

Cross Forma fait travailler les muscles des jambes et de la partie supérieure du corps, en permettant de brûler plus de calories que tout autre exercice. Le mécanisme spécial « long stride » garantit l'ampleur du mouvement pendant l'exercice, avec un équipement indiscutablement compact.

SPECIFICATIONS

Contact	www.technogym.com
Price	From € 4,400
Special features	The only professional cross trainer that can be used in your lounge

MOMENTS OF HI TECH

Technology and "gadgets and gizmos" are frequently sought-after items "for him". However, today it's not enough to simply be aware of the latest technology or have the latest MP3. For those who truly have a lavish lifestyle and high status, the sought-after goals are the most sophisticated mobile phone on the market, or the latest sound system of the most exclusive brand. These items set the owners apart, are proof that they lead outstanding lifestyles. This chapter will display just some of the most exclusive items in the market today. Handmade musical equipment, gold mobile telephones... are some of the examples we have chosen. These items contribute to the creation of an atmosphere of sophistication and luxury for the lucky few.

La tecnología y los conocidos *gadgets* and *gizmos*, acostumbran a ser objetos de deseo para el hombre. Pero actualmente ya no basta con conocer la tecnología o poseer un aparato MP3 de última generación. Para quienes realmente llevan una vida fastuosa y disfrutan de un alto estatus, poseer el teléfono móvil más sofisticado del mercado o el último equipo de música de la marca más especializada es un objetivo asequible. Estos aparatos contribuyen a marcar una diferencia, a demostrar que se tiene un estilo de vida sobresaliente. En este apartado se presentan algunos de los objetos más especiales y exclusivos que pueden encontrarse en el mercado. Equipos de música hechos a mano, teléfonos móviles de oro... son algunos de los ejemplos destacados. Todos estos artilugios añadirán todavía más sofisticación y excelencia al lujo que rodea a unos pocos privilegiados.

Si la technologie et les célèbres « gadgets and gizmos » restent des objets de convoitise, il ne suffit plus aujourd'hui de s'informer sur les avancées techniques ou de s'acheter un appareil MP3 de la dernière génération. Posséder le téléphone portable le plus sophistiqué du marché ou le dernier matériel audio de la marque la plus spécialisée est devenu un must pour ceux qui aiment le faste et occupent une position sociale élevée. Ces appareils contribuent à marquer la différence dans la mesure où ils sont l'expression d'un certain style de vie. Les pages suivantes présentent du matériel audio fait main et des téléphones portables en or, quelques exemples seulement parmi les produits les plus luxueux du marché. Autant d'accessoires qui ajoutent encore à la qualité et à la sophistication dont les rares privilégiés aiment à s'entourer.

GOLDVISH ILLUSION

The Goldvish telephone range is the most luxurious in the world. The flat design comes in various models: yellow, pink or white gold, with the option to set with diamonds and to accessorize with leather cases available in eight different colors.

La gama de teléfonos GoldVish es la más lujosa del mercado. Con su diseño ultraplano, este teléfono móvil se presenta en distintas versiones: de oro amarillo, rosa o blanco, con incrustaciones opcionales de diamantes y la posibilidad de complementarlo con fundas recambiables de piel en ocho colores distintos.

La gamme de téléphones Goldvish est la plus luxueuse vendue sur le marché mondial. Ces mobiles au design ultraplat existent en plusieurs versions : en or jaune, rose ou blanc et incrustés de diamants sur demande. Ils peuvent être glissés dans des étuis en cuir interchangeables disponibles en huit couleurs différentes.

SPECIFICATIONS

Design	Emmanuel Gueit
Contact	www.goldvish.com
Price	From € 19,500 to € 124,000
Special features	15 different versions ranging from yellow gold to full diamond pave incorporate the latest technological innovations.

NOKIA 8800 SIROCCO GOLD

A mobile telephone born from a combination of the latest technology and luxurious materials, a true status symbol. Its elegant design and white gold finish set this item apart from the rest. Its two mega pixel camera, ergonomic keypad and Bluetooth technology are just some of this award-winning model's features.

Un teléfono móvil que une a sus aplicaciones de última tecnología el elemento de lujo y distinción que lo convierte en un símbolo de estatus. Su diseño elegante y los acabados en oro blanco proporcionan distinción al conjunto. Cámara de 2 megapíxeles, teclado ergonómico y *bluetooth* son algunas de las funciones que ofrece este premiado modelo.

Un téléphone portable qui associe progrès technologiques et design luxueux devient un symbole de statut social pour certains consommateurs. Ce modèle de premier choix doit son élégance en partie à son boîtier en or blanc. Au nombre des caractéristiques techniques de l'appareil figurent une caméra de 2 megapixels un clavier ergonomique et le système *bluetooth*.

SPECIFICATIONS

Design	Nokia
Contact	www.nokia.com
Price	From € 1,300
Special features	Handset incrusted with sapphire-coated, scratch-resistant glass display

BOWERS AND WILKINS CM7

The CM7 is the best loudspeaker system of its generation thanks to four decades of experience in the field of high-level electro-acoustic engineering and the technology developed during the manufacture of the 800 Series. It has an extremely wide band and has remarkable precision.

Gracias a cuatro décadas de experiencia en el campo de la ingeniería electroacústica de alto nivel y a la tecnología desarrollada durante la puesta a punto de la Serie 800, la CM7 es el mejor sistema de altavoces de su generación. Combina una banda pasante tan amplia como pueda desearse y una precisión soberbia.

Quatre décennies d'expérience en matière d'ingénierie électroacoustique de haut niveau ayant conduit à une optimisation du concept de la Série 800 font du CM7 le meilleur système d'enceintes de sa génération. Il intègre une très large bande passante d'une précision exceptionnelle.

SPECIFICATIONS

Design	Bowers and Wilkins
Contact	www.bowers-wilkins.com
Price	From € 1,325
Special features	Wenge, maple and rosewood finishes

MBL REFERENCE LINE SYSTEM

The system is formed by MBL 101E acoustic boxes, MBL 9011 amplifiers, MBL 6010D pream-plifier, a MBL 1611 transformer and CD transport with reference MBL 1621. It is particularly notable due to its holographic, three-dimensional sound which, thanks to its omni-directional diffusion, is similar to a live concert.

Sistema formado por cajas acústicas MBL 101E, amplificadores MBL 9011, preamplificador MBL 6010D, convertidor de MBL 1611 y transporte de CD de referencia MBL 1621. Destaca por un sonido tridimensional holográfico que, gracias a su difusión omnidireccional, es seme-jante a un concierto en vivo.

Ce système se compose d'enceintes MBL 101E, d'amplificateurs MBL 9011, d'un préamplifi-cateurMBL 6010D, d'un convertisseur MBL 1611 et d'un transport de CD MBL 1621. Il se dis-tingue par un son tridimensionnel holographique à diffusion omnidirectionnelle, d'une qualité équivalente à celle d'un concert live.

SPECIFICATIONS

Design	MBL
Contact	www.mbl-germany.de
Price	€ 190,160
Special features	Omni-directional sound diffusion

MBL   CD Lector 1621 A

This piece of equipment, hand-made in Germany, is a real gem. It uses top level electronic and circular topological components to give excellent results in most non-conditioned rooms.

Construido enteramente a mano en Alemania, este equipo es una auténtica joya. Utiliza componentes electrónicos y topologías circulares de máximo nivel para ofrecer resultados de primer orden en la mayoría de las salas normales que no estén acondicionadas.

Fabriqué entièrement à la main et composé de pièces électroniques et de topologies circulaires de la plus haute qualité, cet appareil allemand est un authentique joyau. Il donne d'excellents résultats dans les salles dont la majorité n'est pas équipée du système adéquat.

SPECIFICATIONS

Design	MBL
Contact	www.mbl-germany.de
Price	€ 21,850
Special features	Luxurious polished finish in piano black and 24-karat gold

MARK LEVINSON   40 HD MEDIA CONSOLE

Performance, above all, is the reason for owning a Mark Levinson product. The Nº 40 HD Media Console fulfils that implicit promise. Optimized for perfect musical reproduction as well as the impressive video presentation, it is the optimum media console for the true connaisseur.

Su excepcional rendimiento es la principal razón para elegir un producto Mark Levinson. La Consola Nº 40 HD cumple esta implícita promesa. Optimizada para una reproducción perfecta de música y de imagen, es la consola ideal para el verdadero *connaisseur*.

Sa performance exceptionnelle justifie l'acquisition d'un produit Mark Levinson, celle notamment de la console n°40 HD qui tient toutes ses promesses. Optimisé tant pour un rendu musical parfait que pour une reproduction d'images impeccable, cet appareil de haute qualité s'adresse aux véritables connaisseurs.

SPECIFICATIONS

Contact	www.marklevinson.com
Price	€ 22,000
Special features	Various music and film surround mode processing to provide a multi-channel experience from two-channel material

MARK LEVINSON 436 POWER AMPLIFIER

The 436 amplifier is a perfect and stylish solution for the most discerning music lover. The 400 series provides a wide range of advanced equipment with many integration options. A product that has been awarded by the most scrupulous specialists.

El amplificador 436 es la solución ideal y más elegante para los consumidores de música más exigentes. La serie 400 proporciona una amplia variedad de funciones avanzadas y múltiples posibilidades de integración. Un producto premiado por los especialistas más rigurosos.

L'amplificateur 436 est la solution idéale, la plus élégante également, pour tous les mélomanes. La série 400 propose une grande variété d'appareils de la dernière génération et de multiples possibilités d'intégration. Ce matériel primé est conçu pour les consommateurs les plus exigeants.

SPECIFICATIONS

Contact	www.marklevinson.com
Price	€ 4,800
Special features	A power amplifier that perfectly complements other Mark Levinson equipment

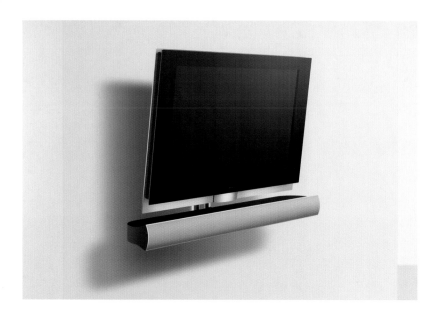

BANG & OLUFSEN BEOVISION 7-40

Beovision 7-40 is one of the most elegant and sophisticated flat screen models in the world. It is manufactured in various sizes and includes many special accessories which allow the screen to turn, even when fixed to the wall. Like the majority of Bang & Olufsen products, it is compatible with elements from other series.

Beovision 7-40 es uno de los modelos de pantalla plana más elegantes y sofisticados del mundo. Se presenta en varios tamaños e integra diversos accesorios especiales para conferir un movimiento giratorio a la pantalla, incluso si se halla instalada en la pared. Como la mayoría de los productos Bang & Olufsen, se puede combinar con otros elementos de distintas series.

Le Beovision 7-40 est l'un des modèles d'écran plat les plus élégants et les plus sophistiqués au monde. Disponible en plusieurs tailles, il intègre divers accessoires permettant de faire pivoter l'écran, même lorsque celui-ci est fixé au mur. Comme la plupart des produits Bang & Olufsen, cet écran est compatible avec des éléments d'autres séries.

SPECIFICATIONS

Design	David Lewis
Contact	www.bang-olufsen.com
Price	€ 9,700
Special features	The new VisionClear technology includes digital filters that accentuate the colors and adapt to the lighting of the atmosphere

BANG & OLUFSEN
HOME THEATER-BeoVision 4

This modular audio and visual solution proposed by Bang and Olufsen includes a plasma screen of up to 65". It can be used with the Beo System Master Unit, which provides all the necessary connections for digital television, BeoLab loudspeakers and auxiliary units.

Esta solución modular de audio y vídeo propuesta por Bang & Olufsen incluye una pantalla de plasma de hasta 65 pulgadas. Se combina con el Beo System Master Unit, que proporciona todas las conexiones necesarias para la televisión digital, los altavoces BeoLab y las unidades auxiliares.

Ce module audio et vidéo, proposé par Bang and Olufsen, intègre un écran plasma 65 pouces. Il est compatible avec le système Beo Master Unit qui fournit toutes les connexions requises par la télévision numérique, les enceintes BeoLab et divers appareils périphériques.

SPECIFICATIONS

Design	Bang & Olufsen
Contact	www.bang-olufsen.com
Price	From € 5,900 to € 13,200
Special features	Home-movie equipment with the best plasma screen on the market

BANG & OLUFSEN
BeoSound 4 Music System

BeoSound 4 is a music system with built-in CD player, FM radio and SD memory card, with the option of digital radio. Music from the radio or CDs can be recorded on an SD memory card directly from BeoSound 4 or transferred to other musical equipment.

BeoSound 4 es un equipo de música con lector de CD, radio FM y lector de tarjetas de memoria flash SD, presentado con la opción de radio digital. BeoSound 4 permite grabar en la tarjeta de memoria SD desde la radio o el CD y escuchar la grabación en el propio BeoSound 4 o en otro equipo de música.

Le système BeoSound 4 comprend un lecteur CD, une radio FM et un lecteur de carte mémoire flash SD. La radio numérique, également disponible en option, permet d'enregistrer de la musique sur une carte mémoire SD depuis la radio ou un CD, laquelle s'écoute à partir de la BeoSound 4 ou d'un autre appareil.

SPECIFICATIONS

Design	Bang & Olufsen
Contact	www.bang-olufsen.com
Price	€ 2,000 (without speakers)
Special features	Musical equipment that is compatible with the whole range of Bang & Olufsen loudspeakers so that music can be heard all over the house

AUDIOME ACCOUSTIC ARMCHAIR

These beautiful leather sofas and armchairs with integrated speakers, which are all reclining and extendable, come in fifty different colors. They are the ideal choice for an atmosphere enveloped by sound waves, offering exceptional quality where listening is concerned.

Estos bellísimos sofás y sillones de piel con altavoces integrados, todos extensibles y reclinables, se presentan en 50 colores distintos. Son la elección ideal para conseguir un ambiente en el que las ondas de sonido envuelven todo el espacio, proporcionando una calidad de audición excepcional.

Ces magnifiques canapés et fauteuils en cuir avec enceintes intégrées, tous extensibles et inclinables, sont disponibles en cinquante couleurs différentes. Un choix idéal pour créer une ambiance sonore qui enveloppe tout l'espace et promet une qualité d'écoute exceptionnelle.

SPECIFICATIONS

Design	Audiome
Contact	www.audiome.fr
Price	From € 3,500 to € 9,450
Special features	Possibility incorporating up to 5 loudspeakers in the same item

MOMENTS OF REGALIA

Watches, fountain pens and sunglasses are the most standard gift items "for him". These are everyday items, with thousands of different models and brands. Yet, how do we define these items when they are limited edition, or made from the most avant-garde materials, or encrusted with diamonds? They become symbols of luxury, of elegance, highly sought after, desirable objects. Although this phenomenon is partly caused by marketing and the mentality of Western society, it is widely accepted that luxurious products are a reflection of class and help to increase social prestige. These items are a step above the rest; they represent exclusiveness and shroud those fortunate few who are able to own them in an aura of sophistication.

Relojes, plumas estilográficas o gafas de sol son los objetos más habituales cuando se habla de regalos para el hombre. Son obsequios comunes, existen miles de modelos y marcas, pero ¿qué ocurre cuando estos objetos se han fabricado con los mejores y más innovadores materiales, cuando tienen diamantes engarzados o, simplemente, se producen en una edición limitada? Ocurre que estos artículos pasan a simbolizar el lujo y la elegancia, y se convierten en objetos codiciados y deseados. No sólo la publicidad y la sociedad occidental lo dejan claro; es de sobra conocido que los productos de lujo realzan la clase y aumentan el prestigio. Estos artículos no son como los demás, pues representan la exclusividad y envuelven a aquellos afortunados que los poseen en un halo de sofisticación y suntuosidad.

Montres, instruments d'écriture ou lunettes de soleil sont les objets offerts le plus couramment aux hommes. Il en existe des milliers de modèles proposés par un grand nombre de marques. Dès lors qu'ils sont réalisés avec les derniers matériaux de la meilleure qualité, sertis de diamants ou simplement fabriqués en nombre limité, ces objets incarnent le luxe et l'élégance, sans manquer de susciter la convoitise. Cela est manifeste dans la publicité et les sociétés occidentales. On sait par ailleurs que le très haut de gamme est le reflet d'un niveau social élevé ou du prestige recherché par certains consommateurs. Ces articles se distinguent de la masse. Ils expriment le faste dont aime à s'entourer une clientèle aisée, soucieuse de rayonner savoir-vivre et bien-être. La plupart d'entre eux ont un petit quelque chose qui les rend pour ainsi dire uniques.

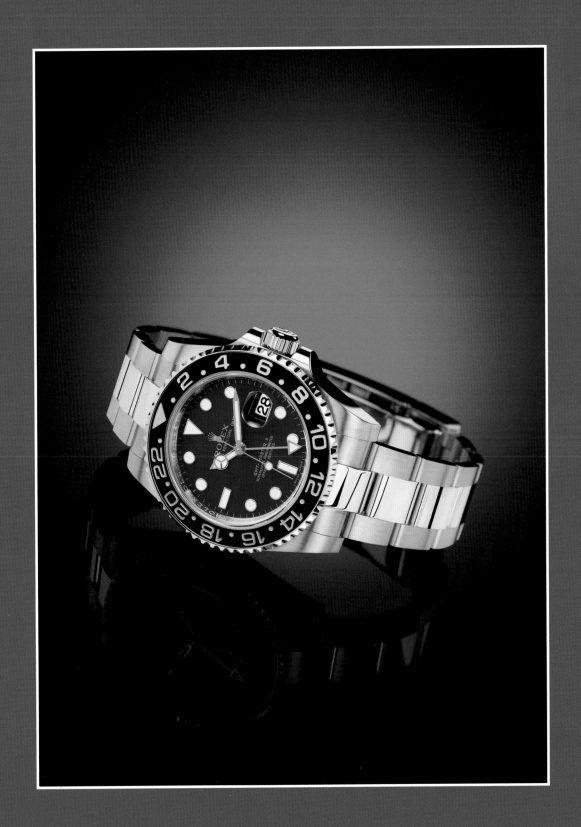

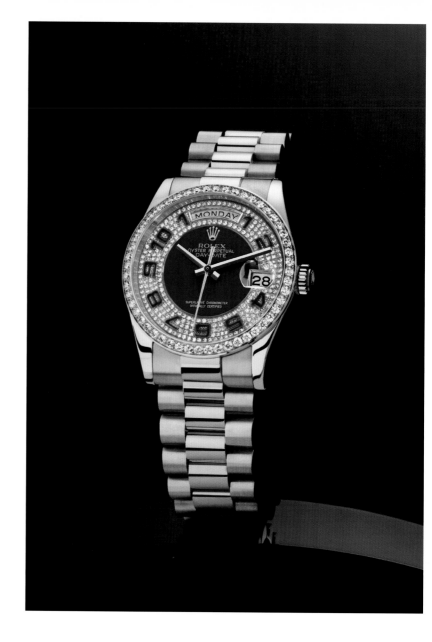

ROLEX OYSTER PERPETUAL YACHT MASTER II
AND OYSTER PERPETUAL DAY-DATE 50TH ANNIVERSARY

These two models are Oyster Perpetual watches. The Yacht Master II chronograph is the first watch to have a programmable countdown feature, designed for regattas. The second model—the Day-Date 50th Anniversary edition Rolex, combines yellow gold with a green decorated dial, the company emblem, a diamond pavé setting, and diamond encrusted edges.

Estos dos modelos son relojes Oyster Perpetual. El Yacht Master II es el primer reloj con dispositivo programable de cuenta atrás, diseñado para las regatas. En el modelo Day-Date 50th Anniversary, Rolex utiliza oro amarillo con esfera lacada de color verde, emblema de la firma, con el pavé de diamantes y el bisel engastado de brillantes.

Voici deux montres Oyster Perpetual de la célèbre marque Rolex. La Yacht Master II est la première dotée d'un dispositif programmable de compte à rebours, conçu pour les régates. Pour le modèle marquant le 50e anniversaire de la Day-Date, le fabricant a utilisé de l'or jaune associé à un cadran laqué vert, à l'emblème de la marque, à un pavé de diamants et à un cerclage serti de brillants.

SPECIFICATIONS

Design	Rolex
Contact	www.rolex.com
Price	€ 24,685 (Oyster Perpetual Yacht Master II) and € 34,610 (Oyster Perpetual Day-Date 50th Anniversary)
Special features	Rolex created the first truly airtight watch in 1926–the Oyster. This primary concept has been a feature ever since

ROLEX GMT-MASTER II

The GMT-Master II features all of Rolex's technological advances. The materials are highly resistant to corrosion and are practically impossible to scratch. Rolex has invented, and patented, an exclusive process to engrave the numbers into the extremely strong material.

El GMT-Master II cuenta con todos los avances tecnológicos desarrollados por Rolex. Los materiales tienen una excelente resistencia a la corrosión y son prácticamente imposibles de rayar. Para grabar los números en este material de extrema dureza Rolex ha inventado y patentado un proceso exclusivo.

La GMT-Master II présente tous les progrès technologiques réalisés par Rolex. Elles est réalisée dans des matériaux très résistants à la corrosion et aux éraflures. Pour graver les numéros dans ce matériau d'une extrême dureté, Rolex a mis au point et fait breveter un processus exclusif.

SPECIFICATIONS

Design	Rolex
Contact	www.rolex.com
Price	€ 17,818
Special features	This watch model is for aviation professionals par excellence. It was christened after the base timeline which marks universal time

GIRARD-PERREGAUX
LAUREATO REGATTA TOURBILLON CHRONOGRAPH WATCH

The Laureato Regatta combines the tourbillon mechanism with exceptional countdown chronometry. It has been designed and developed specifically for competition. A small transparent area on the sphere allows the nobility of its mechanism to be appreciated.

El Laureato Regatta combina un mecanismo tourbillon y un cronómetro dotado con un mecanismo excepcional de cuenta atrás. Se ha diseñado y desarrollado específicamente para la competición. La nobleza de su mecanismo puede apreciarse gracias a una pequeña área transparente en la esfera.

Le Laureato Regatta se compose d'un tourbillon et d'un chronomètre doté d'un mécanisme exceptionnel de compte à rebours. Il a été conçu et fabriqué tout spécialement pour les compétitions. Une petite zone transparente évidée sur le cadran permet d'admirer la noblesse de sa mécanique.

SPECIFICATIONS

Design	Girard-Perregaux
Contact	www.girard-perregaux.com
Price	On request
Special features	This magnificent watch, designed in honor of the thirty-second America's Cup, has been produced in a limited and numbered edition of only 32 units

CARTIER PASHA 42 MM

The Pasha 42 mm watch is presented in various models intended to adapt to the preferences of each client. One of these watches has been prepared with palladium, an innovative avant-garde material. It is a refined metal from the platinum family, very difficult to work with and rarely used in jewelry.

El reloj Pasha 42 mm se presenta en diversos modelos pensados para ajustarse a las preferencias de cada cliente. Uno de estos relojes se ha elaborado con paladio, un novedoso material de vanguardia. Se trata de un metal refinado de la familia del platino, muy difícil de trabajar y raramente utilizado en joyería. Otro de los modelos es de oro rosa de 18 quilates.

La montre Pasha 42 mm existe en différentes versions créées pour répondre au goût de chaque client. L'une des montres ci-contre est en palladium, un nouveau matériau avant-gardiste et très raffiné de la famille du platine, tellement dur à travailler qu'il est rarement utilisé en joaillerie.

SPECIFICATIONS

Design	Cartier
Contact	www.cartier.com
Price	On request
Special features	The different models of the Pasha 42 mm all have the same concept: an exceptional watch that is worn quite naturally

CARTIER TORTUE XL CHRONOGRAPH WATCH

An 18 karat gold tourbillon watch with guilloché silvered dial. The transparent back with sapphire crystal allows observation of the complex watch mechanism. With masculine lines and full grain alligator strap, this watch is a genuine luxury.

Un modelo de reloj con tourbillon y esfera de oro de 18 quilates guilloqueada y plateada. El fondo transparente de cristal de zafiro permite observar el complejo mecanismo del reloj. Las líneas, muy masculinas, y la correa de piel de cocodrilo negra hacen de este reloj un verdadero objeto de lujo.

Ce modèle de montre est doté d'un tourbillon et d'une couronne en or 18 carats, ornée d'un cadran guilloché argenté. Le fond transparent en verre saphir permet d'observer le mécanisme complexe de la montre. Les lignes très viriles et le bracelet en peau d'alligator noir pleine fleur font de cet article un véritable objet de luxe.

SPECIFICATIONS

Design	Cartier
Contact	www.cartier.com
Price	On request
Special features	This watch belongs to a limited and numbered series of 40 examples and is presented in a 950 platinum case

HUBLOT One Million $ BB

This object is the very symbol of the fusion between jewelry and watchmaking. Although similar in lines to the Big Bang, the One Million $ BB conceals a monobloc construction in white gold. A grand total of 493 Top Wesselton baguette diamonds shine with all their splendor without a single setting to be seen.

Esta pieza constituye el símbolo perfecto de la fusión entre joyería y relojería. De líneas idénticas al modelo Big Bang, el One Million $ BB oculta una fabricación monobloque de oro blanco. Los diamantes, 493 piezas de tipo *baguette* de calidad Top Wesselton, brillan con todo su esplendor sin un solo engarce a la vista.

Cet article symbolise à la perfection la fusion entre la joaillerie et l'horlogerie. D'un design identique à celui du modèle Big Bang, le One Million $ BB occulte une fabrication monobloc en or blanc. Les 493 diamants « baguette » Top Wesselton brillent de toute leur splendeur, ne laissant apparaître aucun sertissage.

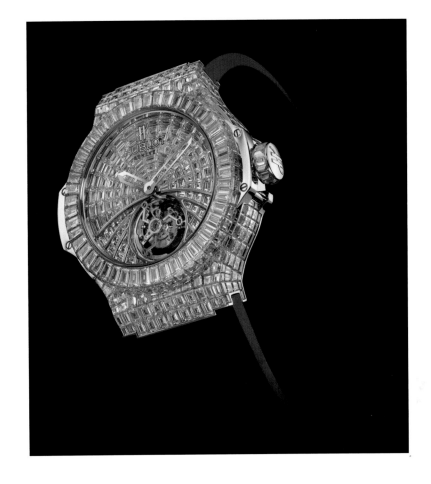

SPECIFICATIONS

Design	Hublot
Contact	www.hublot.com
Price	€ 1,340,000
Special features	The watchmaking brand and the Bunter SA workshop have successfully created a diamond watch with a totally invisible setting

MONTBLANC
TIMEWALKER GOLD MONTBLANC COLLECTION

The Montblanc watch collections are created with the same master craftsmanship used for their writing instruments. This model, with a 1.7" diameter, has an 18 karat pink gold case and a sapphire crystal with antiglare treatment. The chronograph has automatic movement and is COSC certified.

Las colecciones de relojes de Montblanc siguen la misma cuidada artesanía que la utilizada en los artículos de escritura. Este modelo, de 43 mm de diámetro, posee una caja de oro rosa de 18 quilates y un cristal de zafiro con tratamiento antirreflectante. El cronógrafo de movimiento automático posee el certificado de cronómetro oficial (COSC).

Les montres Montblanc sont réalisées avec le même soin artisanal que les instruments d'écriture. Ce modèle de 43 mm de diamètre possède un cadran en or rose 18 carats et un verre saphir anti-reflets. Le mouvement chronographe automatique est certifié par le Contrôle Officiel Suisse des Chronomètres (COSC).

SPECIFICATIONS

Design	Montblanc
Contact	www.montblanc.com
Price	On request
Special features	All Montblanc watches are manufactured in an Art Nouveau style villa built in 1906 in Le Locle, the cradle of traditional Swiss watchmaking

GRAF VON FABER-CASTELL
AMBER FOUNTAIN PEN

The craftsmanship which went into the barrel of this exquisite fountain pen is remarkable. The changing texture and shades make each fountain pen a truly unique and exclusive item; perfect as a gift or for spoiling oneself.

El cuerpo de esta bellísima pluma estilográfica llama la atención por el extraordinario trabajo artesanal con que está realizado. La textura y las tonalidades cambiantes convierten a cada pluma en un preciado artículo único y exclusivo, ideal para regalar o regalarse.

Ce magnifique stylo à plume ne manque pas de retenir l'attention par le design peu ordinaire de son corps réalisé à la main. La matière et les tons chatoyants en font un objet utilitaire unique, luxueux et idéal pour offrir ou se l'offrir.

SPECIFICATIONS

Design	Graf von Faber-Castell
Contact	www.graf-von-faber-castell.com
Price	€ 2,400
Special features	Each of the amber rings has been individually crafted and polished in the workshop and then mounted together with the platinum inlays

CARTIER   LOUIS CARTIER WRITING SET

The limited edition of this fountain and ballpoint pen set further enhances its exclusivity. A treasure that will surely become a heirloom to be handed down the generations. Both pieces are made from platinum and encrusted with black and white lacquer; the nib is made from 18 karat gold and the lid from onyx.

Este juego de pluma y bolígrafo, cuya exclusividad resulta de su edición limitada, se convierte en una joya que de seguro habrá de transmitirse de generación en generación. Ambas piezas son de platino, con incrustaciones de laca blanca y negra; el plumín es de oro de 18 quilates y el capuchón, de ónice.

Cet ensemble composé d'un stylo à plume et d'un stylo à bille, dont l'exclusivité résulte de son édition limitée, devient un bijou qui se transmettra, sans aucun doute, de génération en génération. Les deux accessoires sont en platine incrusté de laque noire et blanche. La plume est en or 18 carats, le capuchon en onyx.

SPECIFICATIONS

Design	Cartier
Contact	www.cartier.com
Price	€ 1,500
Special features	With the classic backgammon motif engraving, this is a limited edition series of 1,850 pieces

GIRARD-PERREGAUX
THE TOURBILLON FOUNTAIN PEN

Girard-Perregaux has resorted to its watch manufacturing experience to produce this fountain pen with square lines. The care placed in the design and in the manufacturing process has resulted in a unique fountain pen in solid gold, with perfect finishes and an original and smooth celluloid texture.

Girard-Perregaux ha recurrido a su experiencia como fabricante de relojes para realizar esta estilográfica de líneas cuadradas. El esmero que se ha puesto en el diseño y en los procesos de fabricación ha dado por resultado una pluma original, de oro macizo, con acabados perfectos y una singular y suave textura de celuloide.

Pour réaliser ce stylo plume à section carrée, Girard-Perregaux a sollicité tout son savoir-faire d'horloger. Le soin apporté au design et les procédés de fabrication ont permis d'obtenir un objet original en or massif, habillé de celluloïd et d'une finition parfaite.

SPECIFICATIONS

Design	Girard-Perregaux
Contact	www.girard-perregaux.com
Price	€ 4,750
Special features	The clip, with a mounted ruby, is inspired in the Tourbillon bridge and has been manufactured by the lost wax casting process

MONTBLANC   ALEXANDER VON HUMBOLDT
(PATRON OF ART LIMITED EDITION)

Alexander von Humboldt is a renowned German naturalist and explorer. This fountain pen has been designed in his honor. The most exclusive materials, such as noble hardwood and black grenadille extol the value of each one of the 4,810 handcrafted pieces, each one with the number of edition engraved in the clip.

Alexander von Humboldt es un célebre naturalista alemán. En su honor se ha diseñado esta pluma. Los materiales más exclusivos, como la madera noble y negra de la grenadilla, ensalzan el valor de cada una de las 4.810 piezas, fabricadas a mano y con su número de edición grabado en el clip.

Alexander von Humboldt est un célèbre naturaliste allemand. Ce stylo à plume, créé pour lui rendre hommage, est fabriqué à partir de matériaux nobles, comme le bois de grenadille noire, qui soulignent la valeur de chacune des 4 810 pièces traditionnellement fabriquées à la main et dont le clip est estampillé d'un numéro d'édition.

SPECIFICATIONS

Design	Montblanc
Contact	www.montblanc.com
Price	€ 1,850
Special features	In 1992 Montblanc instituted the Montblanc de la Culture Arts Patronage Award that coincides with the presentation of the edition Patron of Art

WHITE LAKE   USB Stick

This USB memory stick is not only a utility but also an item of luxury. It is elaborated in 14 or 18 karat gold and has five inlaid diamonds. A highly personal object that can be customized in accordance with the desires of each purchaser.

Un lápiz USB que se presenta no sólo como un objeto útil, sino como un artículo de lujo. Se elabora con oro de 14 ó 18 quilates y tiene cinco diamantes incrustados. Un objeto muy especial que puede ser personalizado según los deseos de cada comprador.

Un objet utilitaire peut être également un article de luxe. C'est le cas de cette clé USB en or 14 ou 18 carats et incrustée de cinq diamants. Un modèle personnalisable suivant le désir du client.

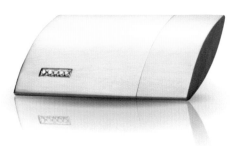

SPECIFICATIONS

Design	Erwin de Vroome
Contact	www.whitelake.com
Price	€ 3,500
Special features	Storage capacity up to 1,024 MB

HR DIAMONDS   Diamond Lighter

Designed by the renowned jeweler Bernard Maquin, exclusively for the Charles Hollander Collection, this lighter is an extremely valuable personal object for daily use, as well as a collectors' item. A unique object, manufactured in 14 karat gold and covered with 33.39 karat black diamonds.

Diseñado por el reputado joyero Bernard Maquin exclusivamente para la Charles Hollander Collection, este mechero es un objeto personal de uso cotidiano de gran valor, así como una pieza de coleccionista. Un objeto único fabricado con oro de 14 quilates y cubierto de diamantes negros de 33,39 quilates.

Créé exclusivement pour la collection Charles Hollander du célèbre joaillier Bernard Maquin, ce briquet est à la fois un objet personnel de grande valeur pour un usage quotidien et une pièce de collection. Il s'agit d'une pièce unique, fabriquée en or 14 carats et sertie de diamants noirs de 33,39 carats.

SPECIFICATIONS

Design	Bernard Maquin
Contact	www.charleshollandercollection.com
Price	€ 18,250
Special features	The choice of black diamonds means that an exclusive deluxe object can be a perfectly valid article for use by men and women

CARTIER LIGHTERS

With each new collection, Cartier presents new designs that reinvent their classic lines. This line of exclusive lighters, made from gold and platinum, enhance the emblematic oval shape of lighters by Cartier.

En cada nueva colección, Cartier presenta diseños que reinterpretan sus modelos clásicos. Esta línea de encendedores exclusivos, de oro y platino, realza las emblemáticas formas ovaladas de los mecheros Cartier.

À chaque nouvelle collection, Cartier présente des modèles qui réinterprètent ses lignes classiques. Celle de luxueux briquets en or et en platine, présentée ci-contre, met en valeur l'ovale emblématique des briquets Cartier.

SPECIFICATIONS

Design	Cartier
Contact	www.cartier.com
Price	From € 2,000
Special features	Stylish, classic and everlasting items. High-quality materials, design and size ensure that they are amongst the favorite personal belongings of any lucky owner

CARTIER BACKGAMMON LIGHTERS

The balance of platinum with black and white lacquer creates a new fusion of materials and textures of great style and sobriety, encased in a contemporary and energetic style that is reminiscent of the Art Deco movement of the 1920s.

La combinación de platino con laca blanca y negra crea un juego de materiales y texturas de gran elegancia y sobriedad, dentro de un estilo moderno y dinámico que recuerda las líneas art déco de los años veinte.

L'association du platine et de la laque blanche et noire crée un jeu de matériaux et de surfaces aussi élégant que sobre. Par leur design, ces briquets rappellent le style Art déco des années vingt.

SPECIFICATIONS

Design	Cartier
Contact	www.cartier.com
Price	From € 1,100
Special features	Remarkable lighters with flawless lines that form part of the Backgammon collection

PRADA SPR57H

The Prada brand denotes high-quality products that fuse an innovative approach with a strong tradition of craftsmanship. This model has an extra-large, mono-lens frame with a sharp, face-hugging shape. The front's metal rim winds seamlessly over the temple, forming a unique triangle decoration bearing the Prada logo.

La marca Prada ofrece productos de alta calidad que combinan un enfoque innovador con una arraigada tradición artesanal. Este modelo monolente extragrande presenta un diseño de líneas decididas y envolventes. El perfil metálico de la parte frontal se prolonga en las patillas formando un original motivo decorativo triangular con el logotipo.

La marque Prada offre des produits de haute qualité qui marient approche novatrice et solide tradition artisanale. Ce modèle de grande taille à un seul verre est très enveloppant. Le profil métallique de la monture se prolonge sur les branches, créant avec le logo un motif décoratif de forme triangulaire d'une grande originalité.

SPECIFICATIONS

Design	Prada
Contact	www.prada.com
Price	€ 180
Special features	Silver, graphite or gold metal is paired with full or graded lenses available in charcoal, bark or green shades

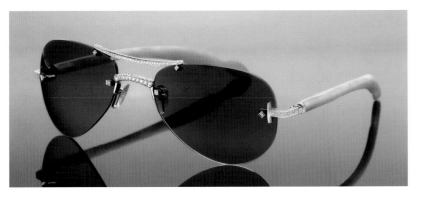

LUXURIATOR SUNGLASSES

Luxuriator sunglasses are the most stylish sunglasses in the world. The combination of exquisite jewelry work and last generation optical technology dictates, rather than follows fashion. It is an object conceived for a new sale's dimension in the most exclusive jewelry stores.

Luxuriator son las gafas de sol más exclusivas del mundo. Una propuesta que avanza ante la moda mediante la combinación de un exquisito trabajo de joyería y la tecnología óptica de última generación. Un objeto concebido para una nueva dimensión de venta en los más exclusivos establecimientos de joyería.

Luxuriator est la paire de lunettes de soleil la plus sélect au monde. Ce produit devance la mode grâce à un délicat travail de joaillerie associé aux derniers progrès de l'optique. Un objet destiné à un nouveau marché dans les bijouteries les plus prestigieuses.

SPECIFICATIONS

Design	Franco Vahe
Contact	www.luxuriator.com
Price	From € 4,100
Special features	Made with diamonds and buffalo horn sidepieces, and available in yellow, white or pink gold

CARTIER SUNGLASSES, SCREW-BASED DECORATION

These sunglasses with the famous rimmed screw motif frame, another famous symbol of the brand, have an oval frame and are available in two sizes with two types of finishes—either gold or brushed platinum. The lenses are polarized.

Las gafas de sol están decoradas con el habitual motivo de tornillo, otro de los iconos de la casa. Presentan una montura frontal ovalada, con acabados en dorado y en platino cepillado, y se hallan disponibles en dos tamaños. Los cristales son polarizados.

Ces lunettes de soleil ornées du motif de la vis, autre caractéristique de la maison, sont constituées d'une monture frontale ovale, à finitions dorées ou en platine brossé, et de verres polarisés. Elles sont disponibles en deux tailles.

SPECIFICATIONS

Design	Cartier
Contact	www.cartier.com
Price	From € 350
Special features	Another item that is an example of the excellence found throughout the entire Cartier product range

PERSOL PO 2656 S (ACETATE SUN)

The Persol 2656 S model was designed in the 1960s. The original four-lens construction combines total protection with a classic and elegant design. This was in fact the model chosen by NASA by virtue of its high protective properties, and subsequently also used for various sporting exploits and high altitude expeditions.

El modelo Persol 2656 S fue diseñado en los años sesenta. La configuración original con cuatro lentes aúna un diseño clásico y refinado con una protección total. De hecho, el modelo fue proporcionado directamente a la NASA por su calidad y elevado nivel de protección, y ha sido protagonista de diversas empresas deportivas y expediciones del máximo nivel.

Le modèle Persol 2656 S, créé dans les années 60 et d'une configuration originale à quatre verres, allie un design classique et raffiné à une protection totale. La NASA apprécie la haute protection de ces lunettes de soleil qui ont participé à des exploits sportifs et à des expéditions en haute montagne.

SPECIFICATIONS

Design	Persol
Contact	www.persol.com
Price	€ 200
Special features	Available in black, tortoiseshell with gray-green lenses and tortoiseshell with brown lenses

CARTIER BACKGAMMON MOTIF CUFFLINKS

A notable feature of these cufflinks are the polished fine lines. Onyx and sterling silver with a palladium finish are common elements in both models; the unique aspect is due to the distinctive shade of lacquer used.

Las líneas depuradas y ligeras definen el diseño de estos gemelos. El ónice y la plata maciza paladiada son elementos comunes en los dos modelos, de modo que el aspecto distintivo resulta del color de la laca.

Ces boutons de manchette se distinguent par un design très épuré. Les deux modèles sont en onyx et en argent massif en plaqué palladium; seule la couleur de la laque les différencie.

SPECIFICATIONS

Design	Cartier
Contact	www.cartier.com
Price	€ 590
Special features	These stylish cufflinks are part of the collection which bears the backgammon board motif. The collection also includes lighters, fountain pens and key rings

CARTIER CUFFLINKS

These sterling silver cufflinks have finishes of the highest quality, sterling silver, or black lacquer and silver with palladium. The engraved motifs are the traditional Cartier designs: oval with double C, the C.A.R.T.I.E.R. motif, etc...

Los gemelos de plata maciza presentan unos acabados de altísima calidad, en los que se utiliza plata rodiada o bien laca negra y plata paladiada. Los motivos grabados son diseños habituales de Cartier: el óvalo con la doble C, el motivo C.A.R.T.I.E.R., etcétera.

Voici des boutons de manchette en argent massif, dont la finition révèle l'excellente qualité : ils sont réalisés en argent rhodium ou en laque noire et en plaqué palladium. Les motifs gravés reprennent les classiques de la marque : un ovale avec un double C, les lettres de C.A.R.T.I.E.R., et cætera.

SPECIFICATIONS

Design	Cartier
Contact	www.cartier.com
Price	From € 500
Special features	The various models of Cartier cufflinks suit an extensive range of tastes and inclinations

CARTIER WALLETS AND CARD HOLDERS

A collection of wallets and card holders, which thanks to its clear pure lines and the satin finish of the leather, makes a classic accessory which is suitable for all ages. Practical and utilitarian, they can be revived again and again without looking out-dated, so that they always look impeccable despite their continuous use.

Una colección de carteras y tarjeteros que, gracias a sus líneas sencillas y al acabado satinado de la piel, se convierten en un accesorio clásico, adecuado para todas las edades. Prácticos y funcionales, nunca resultan anticuados y se mantienen siempre impecables a pesar del uso continuado.

Des portefeuilles et des porte-cartes dont le design sobre et le cuir satiné se marient judicieusement pour donner une collection classique adaptée à tous les âges. Extrêmement fonctionnels, ces accessoires ne portent pas la marque du temps malgré un usage fréquent, de même qu'ils ne passent pas de mode.

SPECIFICATIONS

Design	Cartier
Contact	www.cartier.com
Price	From € 500
Special features	This line of leatherwear is particularly noteworthy for its timeless and elegant design

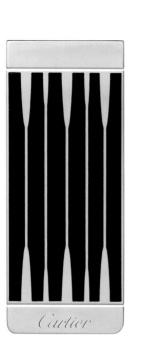

CARTIER MONEY CLIPS

When one wishes to have ones belongings in perfect order and occupying the least space possible, the money clip is ideal. A stylish item, with a resistant and delicate palladium finish.

Estas pinzas para billetes son perfectas si se quiere tener las cosas en orden y conseguir que todo ocupe el mínimo espacio posible. Elegantes objetos acabados en paladio, uno de los metales más resistentes y de delicada textura.

Les inconditionnels de l'ordre et des accessoires peu encombrants apprécient ces pinces à billets, des objets élégants fabriqués en palladium, l'un des métaux les plus résistants et agréables au toucher.

SPECIFICATIONS

Design	Cartier
Contact	www.cartier.com
Price	From € 300
Special features	A small item that is indispensable for meticulous minds

HENK LUGGAGE COLLECTION

Probably the best in the world, the Henk suitcases were devised and created by a team of engineers and designers. They are hand-assembled with technological materials and luxurious pieces. The result is a very exclusive and highly functional piece of equipment.

Probablemente las mejores del mundo, las maletas Henk fueron ideadas y creadas por un equipo de ingenieros y diseñadores. Se montan a mano y están realizadas con materiales tecnológicos y piezas de gran lujo. El resultado es un equipaje exclusivo y altamente funcional.

Probablement les valises les mieux conçues au monde, les articles Henk ont été créés par une solide équipe d'ingénieurs et de designers. Fabriqués main à partir de matériaux technologiques et de pièces de très grande qualité, ces bagages sont aussi luxueux que fonctionnels.

SPECIFICATIONS

Design	Henk
Contact	www.henk.com
Price	From € 13,190 to € 14,670 for leather versions
Special features	More than ten years of research have been necessary to create this extremely strong, yet exceptionally light case

MOMENTS OF DELIGHT

One of the most unique types of pleasure is the pleasure of taste. Tasting is a combination of the senses of taste and smell, with an added impact on touch and sight. The daily enjoyment of the world's best food and drink is an implicit aspect of luxury living. A sumptuous lifestyle should not be without the pleasure of drinking the most exclusive and aromatic wines, or the regular enjoyment of unusual blends and flavors of exclusive products. There is a huge variety of top of the range gastronomic products—it would be impossible to include them all in one book—so we have prepared a selection of traditional products which are most highly regarded by connoisseurs and bon vivants. This small selection includes wines that would be enjoyed by the most discerning sommelier, whiskies made from the best malt and confectionary with unusual textures.

Entre los muchos y variados tipos de placer, uno de los más extraordinarios es el del paladar. Éste convoca y fusiona sensaciones del olfato y el gusto, sin olvidarse de exquisitas percepciones para el tacto y la vista. Una vida de lujo no sería tal sin la posibilidad de disfrutar a diario de los mejores alimentos y bebidas que existen en el mundo. En una vida suntuosa nunca falta el placer de los vinos más selectos, que atrapan con sus aromas. También significa disfrutar habitualmente de los extraordinarios matices y sabores de exclusivos productos. Existen muchos y variados productos gastronómicos de alta gama —sería imposible reunirlos en un libro— entre los cuales hemos preparado una selección de los que se han considerado tradicionalmente productos para sibaritas y *gourmets*. Esta pequeña muestra incluye, entre otros, vinos para satisfacer al más exigente sumiller, *whiskies* elaborados con la mejor malta y bombones de texturas increíbles.

Le plaisir gustatif est peut-être la plus grande source de jouissance que ses différentes perceptions sensorielles offrent à l'être humain. Un produit porté à la bouche sollicite le sens du goût, tout en flattant l'odorat, la vue et parfois le toucher. Une vie de luxe ne serait pas totalement satisfaisante sans l'apport fréquent des meilleurs aliments et des plus délicieuses boissons originaires du monde entier. Tant les grands crus que les produits fins y occupent une place privilégiée. Il existe une telle profusion de produits gastronomiques de grande qualité et couvrant une large gamme de saveurs différentes qu'un livre à lui seul ne suffirait pas pour les présenter en totalité. C'est pourquoi nous nous sommes limités aux plus demandés depuis des lustres par les *gourmets*. Notre échantillon inclut, entre autres, des vins qui raviront le plus exigeant des sommeliers, des whiskies élaborés à partir du meilleur malt, des chocolats surprenants.

TOKAJI ESSENCIA, 1947

The elaboration of this wine, widely referred to as king of wines and wine of kings, is unparalleled. The 1947 vintage is considered one of the best in its history. Its origins are traced back to vines that were left unharvested during the Ottoman invasion in Hungary.

El universalmente conocido como rey de vinos y vino de reyes destaca por su elaboración, única en el mundo. La añada de 1947 se considera una de las mejores de su historia. Sus orígenes se remontan a unas cepas abandonadas en Hungría tras la invasión otomana.

Le tokaj, mondialement connu comme étant le roi des vins et le vin des rois, se distingue par une procédé de fabrication unique au monde. Le millésime 1947 est considéré comme l'un des meilleurs de son histoire. Ce vin hongrois provient de cépages laissés à l'abandon après l'invasion ottomane.

SPECIFICATIONS

Origin	Tokaj-Hegyalja, Hungary
Contact	www.tokaji.com
Price	€ 3,400 approx. (50 cl)
Special features	The first Tokaji late harvest was made: a viscous and extremely concentrated wine, with puréed raisins and currents and other aromas, such as espresso, licorice and ripe fruit

VINHO DO PORTO, 1934

This port wine is prepared exclusively from the grape variety Roriz. The fortification technique consists in the successive interruption of the fermentation process with the addition of ethyl alcohol to the must. The wine remains in the cask for many years and the bottles contain port from just one particular vintage year.

Este vino de Oporto se realiza exclusivamente con la variedad de uva tinta Roriz y su fermentación se va interrumpiendo sucesivamente con el encabezado, una técnica consistente en la adición de alcohol etílico al mosto. El vino permanece durante largos años en la barrica. Las botellas contienen únicamente vino de una añada en particular.

Ce vin de Porto provient exclusivement du cépage Roriz. Sa fermentation est interrompue par le mutage, technique qui consiste à ajouter au moût de l'alcool éthylique. Par ailleurs, il vieillit en fûts pendant de nombreuses années et les bouteilles contiennent uniquement du vin du même millésime.

SPECIFICATIONS

Origin	Bodegas Niepoort, Valle do Douro, Portugal
Contact	www.niepoort-vinhos.com
Price	€ 1,100 approx. (75 cl)
Special features	A perfect port wine to accompany desserts such as autumn fruit or chocolate

PINGUS, 2004

Although this company was only founded in 1995 it has earned a legendary status. These limited production wines are harvested from just 12.3 acres of vineyards. The brilliant Danish oenologist Peter Sisseck is its creator. The wines are concentrated, strong, with a very ripe fruit, an extraordinary balance and ever-greater finesse.

Esta firma, fundada en 1995, se ha convertido ya en un mito. Cinco hectáreas de viñedo bastan para estos vinos de producción muy limitada. El brillante enólogo danés Peter Sisseck es su creador. Los vinos son concentrados, potentes, con aroma de frutas muy maduras, un equilibrio extraordinario y siempre muy sofisticado.

Cette entreprise, fondée en 1995, est devenue un mythe. Seuls cinq hectares de vignoble suffisent pour la production très limitée de ses produits. C'est le brillant œnologue danois, Peter Sisseck, qui est à l'origine de sa création. Il s'agit de vins concentrés et puissants, caractérisés par une note de fruits très mûrs, un équilibre parfait et une finesse sans cesse améliorée.

SPECIFICATIONS

Origin	Dominio de Pingus, Ribera del Duero, Spain
Price	€ 900 approx. (75 cl)
Special features	The harvest is hand-picked during the night, and then the grape is specially selected at the selection table

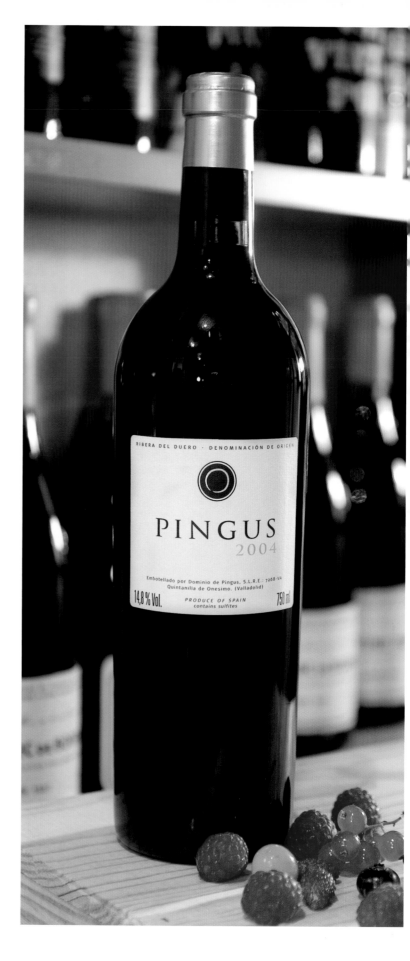

Château
Mouton Rothschild, 1945

The 1945 Mouton Rothschild became the most expensive wine in the world following a legendary auction at Christie's. The vintage year that coincided with the date of the allied victory was one of the best ever and the V on its label has become a mythical symbol. An opulent blend for an unforgettable occasion.

Desde una legendaria subasta en Christie's el Mouton Rothschild de 1945 se ha convertido en el vino más caro del mundo. La añada que coincidió con la fecha de la victoria aliada fue una de las mejores de la historia y la V de su etiqueta se ha convertido en un símbolo mítico. Una combinación de gran opulencia para una ocasión inolvidable.

Depuis sa mémorable vente aux enchères chez Christie's, le Mouton Rothschild de 1945 est le vin le plus cher du monde. Cette vente, qui a coïncidé avec la commémoration de la victoire des Alliés, marquait l'une des meilleures de l'histoire et le V sur son étiquette est devenu un symbole mythique. Ce produit corsé accompagne des événements exceptionnels.

SPECIFICATIONS

Origin	PDO Pauillac, Médoc, Bordeaux, France
Contact	www.bpdr.com
Price	€ 7,000 approx. (75 cl)
Special features	Besides being an indispensable item for the true wine collector, the Mouton Rothschild is distinguished by its distinctive, smooth and mature aromas of dark fruits, coffee, tobacco, mocha and oriental spices

PETRUS, 1990

One of the best vintage years for one of the most famous and prestigious of wines. Petrus is cultivated on the most emblematic 4.6 mi² of essentially clayey soil in the world. The encepagement consists of 96% Merlot and just 4% Cabernet Franc. The harvest is carried out manually and the wine is matured for 20 months in new casks.

Una de las mejores añadas para el más célebre y prestigioso de los vinos. Petrus se cultiva en los 12 km² más emblemáticos del mundo, en un suelo esencialmente arcilloso. El encepe consiste en un 96% de Merlot y tan sólo un 4% de Cabernet Franc. La vendimia es manual y la crianza de 20 meses se realiza en barricas nuevas.

Voici l'un des meilleurs millésimes du plus célèbre de tous les vins. Le Petrus est cultivé sur les légendaires 12 km² de sol essentiellement argileux du domaine le plus prestigieux au monde. Il se compose de deux cépages, soit 96 % de Merlot et seulement 4 % de Cabernet Franc. Le raisin se vendange à la main et le produit vieillit durant 20 mois dans des fûts neufs.

SPECIFICATIONS

Origin	PDO Pomerol, Bourgogne, France
Price	€ 2,700 approx. (75 cl)
Special features	The combination of low acidity and the voluptuous Merlot grape creates a smooth yet majestic mixture, incomparably powerful and rich, with a prodigious longevity

SCREAMING EAGLE, 1999

Screaming Eagle is a deep blend of 88% Cabernet Sauvignon, 10% Merlot and 2% Cabernet Franc. Although it is the most prestigious oenological label in the United States, it is never praised enough by international experts. Its prices soar ever higher in auctions due to its growing prestige.

Una profunda mezcla de Cabernet Sauvignon (88%), Merlot (10%) y Cabernet Franc (2%), Screaming Eagle es la etiqueta más prestigiosa en lo que a enología se refiere en los Estados Unidos, nunca suficientemente elogiada por los expertos de todo el mundo. Por su creciente prestigio, está alcanzando precios cada vez más elevados en las subastas.

Le Screaming Eagle, qui jouit d'une grande réputation aux États-Unis, est obtenu à partir d'un savant mélange de Cabernet Sauvignon (88 %), de Merlot (10 %) et de Cabernet Franc (2 %). Alors que les experts internationaux ne l'ont jamais apprécié outre mesure, il connaît un prestige croissant qui ne cesse de faire grimper son prix dans les ventes aux enchères.

SPECIFICATIONS

Origin	Oakville AVA, Napa Valley, CA, USA
Contact	www.screamingeagle.com
Price	€ 2,500 approx. (75 cl)
Special features	A dense wine with an exceptionally pure opulence and persistent aromas of crème de cassis, characteristic floral hints, and with unmistakable mineral notes

KRUG VINTAGE, 1985

This 1985 Vintage is the jewel of the Krug wine cellars. The first bottle was opened to celebrate New Years Eve 2004 after years in the wine cellar at a controlled temperature. It is distinguished by its diminutive, almost imperceptible, but persistent bubble and its delicate ancient gold color with greenish strokes.

El Vintage de 1985 es la estrella de las bodegas Krug. La primera botella se abrió para celebrar el fin de año de 2004, después de muchos años de bodega a temperatura controlada. Se distingue por sus diminutas, casi imperceptibles, pero persistentes burbujas y por su delicado color de oro antiguo con pinceladas verdosas.

Son millésime 1985 fait la fierté des caves Krug. La première bouteille, ouverte à l'occasion de la Saint-Sylvestre 2004, avait vieilli de nombreuses années dans une cave à température contrôlée. Ce vin se distingue par des bulles minuscules, presqu'imperceptibles mais pétillantes, et par sa délicate couleur vieil or aux reflets verdâtres.

SPECIFICATIONS

Origin	Clos du Mesnil, Champagne, France
Contact	www.krug.com
Price	€ 750 approx. (75 cl)
Special features	Fruity and creamy flavor with slight hints of minerals. An addictive and surprising wine and the masterpiece of the Krug wine cellars

GRAND CRU MONTRACHET, 2002

This exceptional Chardonnay evokes maximum expression, with obvious aromas of honey, aromatic herbs, resin and white pepper, and an essence of ripe, tropical fruit. Although the harvest of ripe grapes from the vine has resulted in an unexpectedly dense wine, it has little aromatic and structural heaviness.

La uva Chardonnay es elevada a su máxima expresión gracias a este caldo excepcional, con ostensibles aromas de miel, hierbas aromáticas, resina y pimienta blanca, todo envuelto en una esfera de frutos maduros y tropicales. La vendimia de la uva madurada en la cepa proporciona un vino de una densidad sorprendente que, sin embargo, se distancia de toda pesadez aromática o estructural.

Le Chardonnay révèle toute sa qualité et son équilibre dans ce cru exceptionnel qui se distingue par de nets arômes de miel, d'herbes aromatiques, de résine, de poivre blanc, auxquels se mêle un goût de fruits exotiques bien mûrs. Le raisin cueilli à maturité donne un vin riche mais léger et à la saveur discrète.

SPECIFICATIONS

Origin	Domaine de la Romanée-Conti, Bourgogne, France
Price	€ 2,200 approx. (75 cl)
Special features	Well-balanced, luminous and exuberant. A risk that has triumphed. Perfect with creamy cheeses

DeLafée

DeLafée is a pleasure for the senses, an exquisite mix of cocoa grains from Ecuador, Venezuela and Ghana. The DeLafée chocolates are ideal for enjoyment of a very sensual experience: chocolate and edible 24 karat gold flakes that shine like stars.

DeLafée es un placer para todos los sentidos, una mezcla exquisita de granos de cacao de Ecuador, Venezuela y Ghana. Los bombones DeLafée son la combinación ideal para disfrutar de una experiencia muy sensual: chocolate y copos de oro comestibles de 24 quilates que brillan como estrellas.

DeLafée, un délice pour tous les sens humains, consiste en un mélange exquis de fèves de cacao d'Equateur, du Venezuela et du Ghana. Les assortiments de chocolats DeLafée garantissent une expérience des plus sensuelles grâce à des copeaux d'or comestibles de 24 carats, brillants comme des étoiles, incorporés au chocolat.

SPECIFICATIONS

Origin	www.delafee.com
Price	From € 27
Special features	DeLafée Chocolate combines two of the most luscious and sensual pleasures in the world: the finest Swiss chocolate and 24-karat edible gold

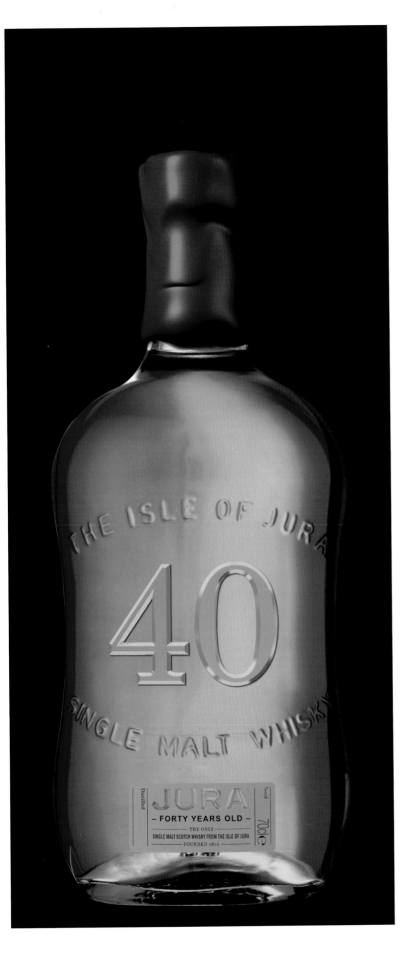

THE ISLE OF JURA 40 YEARS OLD

A mystical island with soft sea breezes is found off the west coast of Scotland. The island's malt whisky distillery produces a genuine gift of nature. This delicate and sublime malt whisky is a product of the pure and fresh island air, the spring water and the mark left in the distillery by generations of craftsmen.

En la costa este de Escocia se encuentra una isla mágica de suaves brisas marinas. Su destilería de *whisky* de malta da vida a un regalo de la naturaleza. El aire puro y fresco, el agua de manantial y las generaciones de artesanos de la destilería crean un *whisky* de malta delicado y sublime.

Une île féérique baigne au large des côtes Est de l'Écosse, délicatement balayée par les brises marines. Le *whisky* malt produit dans sa distillerie est un véritable cadeau de la nature. L'air pur et frais, l'eau de source et le savoir-faire de plusieurs générations ont donné naissance à un *whisky* de malt absolument délicieux.

SPECIFICATIONS

Origin	www.thedalmore.com
Price	€ 1,920 (70 cl)
Special features	Distilled and filled to cask on 12th November 1966 by Richard Paterson and the men of Jura

COHIBA BEHIKE

These cigars were prepared to commemorate Cohiba's 40th anniversary. The plants were hand-picked from the seedbed, and the meadows where they grew and the vegueros who cultivated them were also carefully selected. The tobacco was aged for between 5 and 6 years. Norma Fernández, the most experienced *torcedora* of El Laguito, the legendary Cuban tobacco factory, supervised the production.

Estos puros se elaboraron para conmemorar los 40 años de Cohiba. Las plantas se seleccionaron desde el semillero, también se escogieron las vegas donde crecieron y los vegueros que los cultivaron. El añejamiento del tabaco fue de entre cinco y seis años. La manufactura corrió a cargo de Norma Fernández, la torcedora más veterana de El Laguito, la legendaria fábrica de tabaco cubana.

Pour la fabrication de ces cigares à l'occasion des 40 ans de Cohiba, les plants de tabac ont fait l'objet d'une rigoureuse sélection dans la pépinière ainsi que les sols dans lesquels ils ont été repiqués et les paysans qui les ont cultivés. La maturation des feuilles s'effectue sur 5 ou 6 ans. La célèbre manufacture de tabac cubaine El Laguito a remis à Norma Fernández, la plus ancienne employée, le soin de rouler tous les cigares.

SPECIFICATIONS

Origin	www.altadis.com
Price	€ 15,000 (case with 40 cigars)
Special features	The Cohiba Behike is the world's most expensive and exclusive pure cigar, with only 4,000 cigars prepared in batches of 40 units. The cigars holders were designed by the Parisian firm Elie Bleu

Special thanks to

We would like to give a special thanks to the following collaborating firms. Without their generous help this book would not have been possible.

Aviation Images (www.aviation-images.com)
Equipo singular (www.equiposingular.es) for Luxottica
Netjets (www.netjets.com)
Purple (www.purplepr.com)
Vila Viniteca (www.vilaviniteca.es)

Photo credits

Photos pgs. 214 to 219 © Aviation Images
Photos pgs. 321 to 327 © David Whittaker
Photos pgs. 389 to 397 © Marc Llibre Roig

The remainder of the photographs shown in this book have been generously loaned by the collaborating firms.